THE SQUID WEEKLY
VOLUME ONE

BEN RIETEMA

The Squid Weekly Volume One by Benjamin Rietema

Published by Westernesse Press

Boulder, CO 80301

www.thesquidweekly.com

© 2017 Benjamin Rietema

ben@thesquidweekly.com

ISBN: 978-0-9996856-0-0

For my parents

CONTENTS

1-800-HEAVEN

Welcome to the 1-800-HEAVEN hotline. All prayer calls are recorded for quality-assurance purposes. Please visit our website at cash4salvation.org or one of our offices in Nebula Six. Business hours are from 9 am to 9:25 am every other Tuesday, alternating every two and a half months beginning in 33 AD.

For Christianity, press one. For Judaism, press two. For Islam, press three. For Atheism, please hang up and try again. If you hold to no religion or your religion is not listed, please convert and try again.

[1]

Thank you for choosing Jesus Christ. We hope to resolve your issue shortly. Please enter your denomination using the alphanumeric keypad on your phone followed by the pound key.

[6, 7, 6, 4...]

Thank you for choosing Evangelical Southwestern Re-reformed Mumbling Buttlickers. To confess a sin, press one. To beg for the salvation of a loved one, press two. To request the damnation of an enemy, press three. To request divine favor for your athletic team, press four. To make a deal with God, press five. To tell God what you really think of him, press six. To thank God for providing in a time of need, press seven. To question why God did not provide in a time of need, press eight. To make someone love you, press nine. To make someone stop loving you, press ten. To contest your afterlife placement, press eleven. Press twelve to hold for a heavenly representative.

[12]

Before I connect you with a qualified representative, I need to ask you some questions. From your birth to the present, how many times have you doubted your faith? Please note that any number but zero may delay the time in which your request is processed.

[0]

Thank you for your honesty. Please estimate the number of lies from your birth to the present, not including lies told to children under the age of three.

[…]

Great. We're almost there. Just a few more questions. Do you hold to those precepts as established by the second council of Nicaea of 787 AD or those of the Council of Hieria of 754? Press one for Nicaea. Press two for Hieria.

[…] [2?]

Thank you. Under the Augustinian precept of free will wherein God has chosen to make a human species which has the ability but not the prerequisite of choosing a freedom wherein they may take a course of action prescribed by faith or that prescribed by heresy and herein marginalize the role of God's omniscience and omnipotence while emphasizing the liberty of the human species (*Homo sapien*) over said Almighty power, did this give you the ability if not the right to pretend to love Candice Josephson in the fifth grade in order to obtain her slice of pepperoni pizza, hereby knowing that said action would elicit immeasurable pain for said person after said pizza was eaten and said love was found to be simulated? Press one for yes. Press two for no.

[...] [2?]

Thank you. Please clearly state the greatest sin you have committed.

[...] Cheating ... on my wife.

I'm sorry but I can't understand what sin you committed.

Sleeping with other women.

You have selected: parking ticket violation. Is this correct? Press one for yes. Press two for no.

[2]

Please try again. Please say your sin.

Cheating on...

You have selected: murder of a trusted friend. Is this correct? Press one for...

[2]

Please try again. Enter...

CHEATING...

You have selected: taking kickbacks from an international drug cartel. Is this correct? Press one for yes. Press two for no.

[1]

Thank you. I'm sorry but all of our heavenly representatives are occupied. Hold time: fifty-nine years, two months, and twenty days. We appreciate your patience. Someone will be with you shortly.

[Shrill Christmas Music]

THE GREAT AIR-CON

"Join the United States in air conditioning the world… No really." This will be the 2037 slogan for a controversial initiative to cool the planet—and to massively increase the sale of air conditioners, ice cubes, fans, and albums by the rapper Ice Cube. Among other things, the US government will encourage individuals to direct A/C units outdoors, stating "if everyone cools the outside, then no one will have to cool the inside because of science."

Unfortunately, many air conditioning units will also issue toxic radiation at random intervals, due to blocks of plutonium being haphazardly nailed to the side of each unit. The "solution" will cool the planet by one hundred and twenty degrees and encase ninety percent of the US in five feet of ice. Polar bears will breed to the point where they gain political clout and seize much of the eastern seaboard as "payback."

President Chimp, who will furiously debate golden retriever Daisy in the 2032 election, will head the initiative. Top scientists will express anger and bewilderment, claiming that the "Great Air-Con" violates the basic rules of physics and will increase the world's warming. In an audacious move, President Chimp will offer to groom scientists and then proceed to destroy the Oval Office in what his aides have dubbed his "creative process."

Nominee Daisy will have a strong run, buoyed by her adorable, fun-loving nature and near constant enthusiasm to chase any thrown object. Ultimately, she will lose at the polls, mostly because of an inability to tell the difference between an al-Qaeda terrorist and an American marine, instead labeling both as "the sort who might feed me food under the table."

Daisy will also capitulate to any interest group with Tasty Bits dog treats, which brings trouble when she supports the United American Racist Front and Balloons For All, an organization that provides orphans with one red balloon. Pundits, politicians, sound bite technicians, and Daisy's owner Fred will agree that Balloons For All is a pretty worthless charity, almost as bad as investing in a college education in 2032.

Most universities will be sponsored by fast food corporations, and every job will be offered on a first-come-first-served basis due to the immense increase in discrimination lawsuits. All groups will be protected, except upper-class white males, who will be required to spend five hours per day in a cardboard box begging for forgiveness. None will be forthcoming.

The Great Air-Con will not be the last of an eight-year period of American history some will call "The Amazing Chimp-tastrophe." In a move that will stun even his most avid supporters, President Chimp will funnel government assets into the implementation and growth of rainforest-type environments.

Asked whether this would damage the American economy, seeing as no quality rainforest can actually be grown in the US—or anywhere due to the enormous ice fields covering most of the planet—President Chimp responded that he was unaware of any problems in his plan, rather tweeting, HOOO HOOO HAAA HAAA HAAAA.

White House Press Secretary translated this to mean, "I understand and respect views different from mine, and this plan will not be implemented without full Congressional approval." Two hours later, Big Ape New Awesome New Attraction will be initiated, and many will agree the acronym B.A.N.A.N.A. may have been forced.

Convincing President Chimp to let go of B.A.N.A.N.A. will be the last of White House worries, however. Presidential aides will spend most of their time preventing him from seeing *Planet Of The Apes*, whose plot line he will understand but whose fiction he will not. His cabinet will be half primates and half humans, who will argue ceaselessly over the proper place to defecate. Compromise will be reached to use the East Wing or—if that is not possible—ornamental pots placed at intervals around the White House.

It will be a strange time for the United States. Fifteen A/C units per household will be the new social norm. Smart phones will eat little Johnny's homework and little Johnny, and a monkey will be president. But no one will blink an eye because it's all fake news. Only fools believe in the truth. And when a chimpanzee with more rights than a US citizen has designated your house as a new getaway for him and his chimp pals, denying reality might be the only thing to get you by.

MORDOR VACATION

Wish you could escape to a place that stays a balmy hundred and five year-round with no vegetation or water? Come on over to Mordor, a land where conservation is a joke and recycling sure isn't what you think it is. Formerly closed off as too dangerous and genocide-y, Mordor is the new Cuba, the untouched paradise for the adventurous tourist.

As rightful ruler of Middle Earth with a penchant for fascism, Lord Sauron welcomes all to his humble abode, ensuring everyone that the whole "enslaving the world thing" was a simple misunderstanding. Flights from Isengard to the capital of Barad-dûr go for less than $69 one way. Spirit Airlines, the regional provider for Mordor, even offers frequent flyer programs for people who can't get enough of those wonderful sulfuric fumes.

From the tortured plains of Gorgoroth to the only continually active volcano in Middle Earth, you will find the perfect barren wasteland to bring the family. We like to say it's like Los Angeles with less of a gang problem.

Meet locals who will let you sample native delicacies like raw mutton, maggoty bread, and select appendages of the weakest member of their community. ***Traveler's tip: Don't*** *be the weakest, or you might end up on the menu!* It's prison rules here, so make sure to assert your dominance and challenge the most threatening resident in hand-to-hand combat. If you win, you'll make some friends—or at least enemies who will keep their distance until your back is turned.

If you've never met a creature with a brain made for smashing and not necessarily for linguistic capabilities, this is your chance. We'd love to introduce you to a troll with a single syllable name like Bill, Tom, Joe, or Trump. Confuse one with simple math problems, and the hilarity will follow.

While you're in Mordor, make sure to tour the fortress at Barad-dûr, where you can view our legendary spawning pits and real prisoners being tortured for information. You can even watch as we incite our community to bloodlust, then equip them with primitive weapons and send them to burn down some innocent villages.

Stop at Nine Rings Gift Shop before you leave and pick up some pro-slavery magnets and a mug in the shape of a volcano. It's our Mordor promise that someone was exploited in the making of your product, maybe even one of your relatives. Grab a postcard there and mail it to family members with a quick ransom note. Try to sound desperate, otherwise you might not ever get home!

Opportunities to get outside and see the local wildlife abound in Mordor. See animals such as fell beasts, horses with red eyes, wolves, wargs, elephants who like to stomp, and spiders. The spiders in particular like to pose for photos—but be careful because they'll jab you with their stinger. **Traveler's Tip:** *Remember to pack an adventurous spirit and a can of mace!*

Stay in authentic mud-covered huts at a bed and breakfast or in a barracks where a friendly four o'clock wake-up call is provided free of charge. Work with select members of the community in their daily tasks like digging trenches, digging pits, or digging for the sake of digging. Talk about meeting your daily exercise goals!

Have no trouble getting around when you can rent a member of our community to carry you wherever you'd like. And if they break down or threaten to eat one of your legs, we promise to replace them within twelve hours. We even provide a hefty knife to fend them off in the intervening time.

So, at the end of your trip, don't be surprised to hear your kids say, *Thanks for the great trip, respected authority figure! I learned how to butcher a person in less than five minutes and why a free market economy is just plain silly. Plus, that skin rash will always remind me of what an awesome time we had. Can we go back again next vacation?*

Yes. Yes you can, little maggot.

ALPHA MALE

Follow these steps and instantly be on your way to ALPHA MALE DOMINANCE. Don't question anything, not your choice in underwear, not your ability to run a country. Big words are confusing and allow for nuance. Nuance? Alphas live in a yes or no world. Yes, I would like to purchase shady oil contracts from unstable dictatorships. No, do not give me a pamphlet for saving the blue whale.

So, instead of complicated words use small words like BOMB, BEER, BOOM, BAM, WAA-POW, and SMASH. Only refer to women as SHE-BEASTS. They respect this use of language, as well as picking up their personal objects with greasy hands and putting them down in the wrong place.

A perfect alpha male expression would be: BAM! ME WANT SMASH BOMB BEER SHE-BEAST. This works on many levels. It could mean "I would like to impregnate a woman and/or procure cheap liquor," "I am a potential terrorist and this place seems to have the right amount of women and children," or "Could you direct me to the nearest NRA gathering?"

For an Alpha, there is NO NEED for conjunctions or

clarification. The urine marking the chair means that chair is *always taken*. The lamp is broken because talking through problems is hard. The animal carcass out back was a caribou, and it increases the property value.

Walk with a long stride and a purpose, and carry a LARGE, BLOODY KNIFE to heighten the suspense. Pay attention to these things especially when you have lost something. Nothing says dominance like an alpha with a sharp object striding in circles, franticly looking under tables, and muttering. It means, "I sense a wounded female deer was here three hours ago."

Bodily appearance as an Alpha is important. Some people believe that the body is composed of many parts, but as an Alpha, this just isn't true. Sixty percent of the body is chest, twenty-eight percent is arms, and two percent is brain. As a rule, the brain is useful primarily to remember not to shit yourself.

If at all possible, sharpen your canine teeth and have a raw leg of mutton on your person at all times. This skips many social pleasantries to get to the main point. Nothing says "I have large genitalia" more than tearing into a dead sheep while barely clothed.

Using your physicality to express your prowess is key because at ~~some~~ ~~most~~ almost all points in the Alpha's life, he will desire to PROCREATE. To do this he must create a nest composed of discarded newspaper, bright pieces of ribbon, and powerful sedative drugs. Once a she-beast is impressed or merely feels pity, the Alpha can consummate the TENDER ACT OF LOVE, deny any emotional connection, and leave forever.

DO NOT "fall in love" in this process. Fall in love and months later an Alpha will have six pups, a thirty-year mortgage, and a job impressing tourists at the Toronto Zoo. No more running in the woods without clothes; no more taking down a full-grown mule deer on a Saturday. His rippled muscular form will become a podgy, listless fur ball sucking up and paying taxes. Alphas DON'T PAY TAXES. Alphas COLLECT TAXES through fraud, racketeering, and good, old fashioned extortion.

All these could be yours. Being an Alpha is a process that begins and ends RIGHT NOW. Join the elite that inhabit those hallowed halls: the fearless wolf pack leader Grimm, Mongol warlord Genghis Khan, the feared serial killer "Man-Crusher," and Jim from accounting.

Some may say the era of the Alpha has ended, that teamwork and compassion are the rules of the game. Life is not a game—unless that game is *RUTHLESS DOMINANCE*. Life is natural selection, evolution, where you must protect your right to drink first at the watering hole and stare down everyone you meet.

One need only consider the alternatives to being an Alpha: weakness, ordering vegetarian, respecting people in service professions, holding doors open, empathy, voting Democrat. But as an Alpha, act now and think only when the police ask about that missing hiker.

You have no time to waste. BEAT LIFE. BEAT DOWN YOUR ENEMIES. BEAT DOWN YOUR FRIENDS. BECOME AN ALPHA NOW.

THE MIGHTY SEAGULL

Long has the mighty seagull kept its prized spot at the top of the scavenging pack—picking through sandy Doritos and half-eaten sandwiches, crapping on tourists, and occasionally suffocating on a plastic bag. And, rightly enough, the seagulls are proud of their country and of their origins—the legendary dodo, whose only flaw was being a small, flightless bird who didn't do enough cardio.

In US history, seagulls have consistently made it into *Forbes'* "Top Ten Birds To Have Changed Society," and only three years ago, Lamar Birdsley graced the cover of *Time* magazine as the seagull covered in oil slick. Birdsley was later admitted into the Avian Hall Of Fame, whose other members include Toucan Sam, Big Bird from *Sesame Street*, and the bird hit by a Randy Johnson fastball.

But the plight of white seagulls is under attack. Green Peace initiatives to help endangered birds and affirmative action programs are taking place across the country. The sudden influx of pigeons, herons, robins, sparrows, and that overly large seagull with the wandering eye has left gulls at a crucial junction.

Gulls fear what they stand to lose: the overcrowding of their beach, avian welfare, and the loss of their traditions, only to be replaced by big city birds who care little for small town fowl. What does a pigeon know of beach life? Strolling unheeded into rush hour traffic, extorting politicians, and holding up passerby for leftover food—these are things rural gulls don't want to know anything about.

Thus, seagulls have united in the Avian Educated White Male Association For National Birds Everywhere (But Mostly For Seagulls) (abbrev. A.E.W.M.A.F.N.B.E. (B.M.F.S.)). This organization seeks to influence Congress through peaceful means but will fly into airplane engines, expel feces on the president's motorcade, and stare in a disconcerting way if necessary.

The association's first goal is to garner public support. To these ends, gull advocates have adopted the tactics of Save The Children and Green Peace, and circulate seafood markets and outdoor malls, cawing obnoxiously whenever individuals with food are present. Unfortunately, most advocates were yelled at or shooed off with newspapers, much like their non-profit counterparts.

On the political side, the association has focused on government officials. Only yesterday, a seagull lobbyist received the last of a Fritos bag from Senator Johnson of Louisiana. This is progress, and the director of

A.E.W.M.A.F.N.B.E. (B.M.F.S.) believes the seagull community can expect his vote when the bill goes to Congress.

What exactly is in this bill? Generally, the legislation aims to make anything with seagull feces on it to be seagull property and for more cracker-orientated snacks to be made available. The gulls also want more government support of the working class, especially unemployment benefits for gulls who fly into windows.

To gather momentum, seagulls have also engaged the Facebook, Twitter, and Instagram audience. Most posts involve blurry photos of water and buoys, obscure leftist rants, and tweets consisting of the letter "g" one hundred and forty times. However, the Facebook page has more than two million followers, many of whom are Millennials who think they are supporting a startup clothing company called GULL. The fact that no apparel or any mention of clothing can be found on the page has not dissuaded these ardent followers.

The organization seeks to have legislation in place by 2020, but like many groups, its goals will certainly change as time goes on. A focus on the seagull community may easily slide to an extreme white bird nationalism and vicious attacks on any creature that doesn't find raw fish guts appealing. Or gulls could embrace their fellow avian and form a united front for the reduction of bird heart disease from unhealthy fast food. Time can only tell where A.E.W.M.A.F.N.B.E. (B.M.F.S.) will go.

IF HUMANS WERE BEARS

If humans were as large as bears, driving would be awful, especially for people who bought those electric smart cars. They could be renamed "dumb cars" or "thoroughly inconvenient cars," seeing as some people would have their feelings hurt if they were driving a dumb car. It would be funny to drive a dumb car, however. If the power steering didn't work or the A/C started blasting in the middle of winter, the owner couldn't complain. They were the idiot who bought a dumb car.

Of course, other pressing questions come up too: Can tires take the stress of a bear in the driver's seat? Or would they just blow up? Would everyone start driving around in circles? Would cup holders become irrelevant? These questions could be tested by scientists with real bears and there could be a TV show and it would be really interesting. Any show's worth would increase tenfold with the addition of a bear, especially anything involving politics.

Reporter: *Mr. President, you've answered this question before. Now, however, with a live Kodiak brown bear in attendance, how would you respond to environmental concerns? Do take into consideration that recent legislation has severely restricted the annual salmon run and polluted this bear's natural habitat, and "Pauly" here has eaten the last two politicians whose answers he didn't like.*

Look at it this way: Politicians could either wrestle a nine-hundred-pound mammal or the government would function around appeasing bears, both of which would be significantly more interesting than the government today. Probably not better, but definitely more interesting.

If people *were* bears, however, instead of being as big as them, lives would change significantly. People would suddenly weigh a ridiculous amount and still be able to run forty miles-per-hour, which is faster than Usain Bolt, whom we could rename Usain Not-So-Fast-Anymore or Food, for short.

So, forget AA and the job, ditch the support group and the therapy, give up drugs and relax as one of the largest mammals in existence. Life now consists of uninterrupted sleep for half the year and eating astronomical amounts of fish the other half. And yeah it'd be bad if someone didn't like salmon, but after eating fifty pounds of it per day, it probably wouldn't matter anyways. Plus, if anyone got tired of the whole fish thing, they could always take down a caribou.

The potential for mauling people alone would more than make up for the bothers of driving. Instead of threatening violence, people could follow through, and no one could blame anyone because we are bears and that's kind of what bears do. Occasionally some virtuous soul might want to throw morality and standards of decency around, maybe suggest counseling or a spa retreat.

Reacting violently to problems is really hurtful, they'd say in a calm, psychiatric voice as they laid a hand on your vast paw. *You can't go around tearing people's legs off whenever they make you angry or sad. You have to talk through your struggles. Learn to react rationally and calmly... You know what? It's probably all that gluten in your diet. And you hardly exercise... Yoga, you should try yoga.* It'd be great because you could eat them too.

Bears don't need a dental plan or health coverage. What is someone going to do? Call up Humana and say, "Hello, I'm a bear?" No. Even under Obamacare, bears are barely covered—even then the insurance premiums are ridiculous considering you may have eaten a couple of cans and gained thirty pounds yesterday.

As far as fashion goes, well, instead of pawing through the closet and worrying about colors going together, you could wear the same old knotty rug *every day*, and it'd be okay because everyone else would be wearing the exact same rug. Sure, it might be warm in the summer, but bears spend most of their time in ice-melt, so… no longer a problem.

Of course, there'd be stipulations. Some people don't want to be a bear. They'd have qualms about eating other animals or having such bad breath or living outside or not having a phone or whatever.

But why order pizza when you can walk into Domino's and get as many pizzas as you want? Who needs 911 when you *are* 911? Why call Jenny when she's just going to mention the restraining order? Everything is all right because if you're a bear, everything else is not a bear. And when you're not a bear, well… you just wouldn't understand.

BIRDS AND BEASTS' NEWS REPORT

Moose: This is the Birds and Beasts' News Report—news by wild animals, for wild animals. I'm Jeff Moose.

Deer: And I'm Susan Deer.

Jeff: Good news for scavengers this morning. Heronsley, our reporter in the sky, has informed us that a dumpster behind the Whole Foods has been filled with expired pastries and organic vegetables. The container looks to be unguarded with the lid open. Remember folks that according to new avian regulations, entering grocery stores and defecating on the produce is now frowned upon.

Susan: Now we turn to a sad item in the news. Local prairie dog and mother of eight pups Meredith Henderson has been the victim of a hit and run. Witnesses report that the perpetrator was driving a GMC Yukon and may have accelerated the car in order to hit the crossing animal. According to Meredith's husband, she was crossing the road to forage and possibly dig a hole.

Officer Buck Anderson was the first on the scene and commented that Meredith was "definitely dead" and "smeared beyond all recognition really." Johnny Henderson, recently bereaved of his mother, had this to say,

"Cheep, cheep… cheep, cheep, cheep, cheep. Cheep."

Jeff: Wow. Such wisdom from a two-month-old pup. I think we can all take a lesson from those words, don't you think Susan?

Susan: Truly, Jeff. Truly.

Jeff: In other news, according to leading psychologist and researcher Dr. Bunny Foo Foo, hawk violence is up twenty percent from last spring. *[Cut to Dr. Foo Foo]*

"We've always had testy relationships with birds of prey, but according to recent surveys and data, we've seen around twenty more deaths per week. Before a rabbit could expect to live a relatively peaceful life in Mr. McGregor's vegetable garden, but the outdoors are now filled with fear."

Susan: Rabbit and other hopping communities continue to advocate claw control, citing that claws are only used to disembowel rabbits and contribute to more bunny killings than anything else. Pro-claw hawks argue de-clawing would only take away the tools they need to survive and to protect them from other wild beasts. Concealment experts continue to recommend that in dangerous situations rabbits should lie perfectly still and pretend no one can see them.

Jeff: We turn to our head meteorologist Ed Rooster for

the forecast. What's the weather going to be this week Ed?

Ed: *Cock-a-doodle-doo!*

Susan: Same weather again, huh? It seems we've had a chance of rain, snow, sun, and wind for a while now.

Ed: *Cock-a-doodle-doo!*

Susan: All right, all right. Shut up. Shut up!

Jeff: Today marks the conclusion of a thirty-year study by squirrels. They investigated why the other side of the road looks appealing until a squirrel gets to the middle of the road, at which point the other side looks a lot worse than the side they left. Despite extensive research, results were inconclusive. Some researchers think that the chemical composition of the grass actually changes at the midway point, while others believe it has something to do with the short-sightedness of squirrels.

Susan: Well, Jeff, I think most every animal has experienced the sort of thing squirrels are talking about. But this one will just have to be a mystery, like why approaching headlights are so fascinating.

Jeff: Yep. I hear you there, Susan. Well, that concludes our news report. Remember to stay safe out there wild animals. From the Dowling's back yard, I'm Jeff Moose, biding you a good night.

AMNESIA INTERNATIONAL

Memory loss, it's the new medical treatment that's sweeping the globe. At Amnesia International, instead of doing away with Alzheimer's and other neurocognitive diseases, we have decided to embrace them in the way that the US embraced Russia during WWII—tentatively but with the glossy-eyed hope that yes, this will work if we believe hard enough.

See we're taking a page out of nature's book, the one that's brutal and has trouble with math. But with our help, maybe we can fold that page into a paper airplane or a suave origami crane to impress your friends. They will look at your crane and say, *You're denying your problems exist again, aren't you?* Yes, yes you are.

Our treatment is all about taking perceived negatives and transforming them into positives. The dandelions in your lawn are no longer weeds when you want them there. And when they take over the rest of your lawn, it's like, *Hey, that's totally cool. It's all natural, man.*

We like to call it alternative science, which is like normal science but with green tea extract, Krishna, and a bottle of gin. So, maybe our clinical trials were conducted in a high school lab. And sure, they didn't all go so well, and yeah, maybe we still can't find Kenny. The point is that he seemed really, really happy—far too happy for someone with that many needles in them.

Whatever. The point is that the most powerful antidote to your problems is to forget they exist. Look at all of the happiest people in the world—*retirees*. Who has the hardest time remembering what happened for the first thirty years of their life? *Retirees*. Suddenly playing bingo, losing your car keys, and forgetting to put on underwear sounds really nice, doesn't it?

We've taken these basic facts of reality—retirees, happiness, memory loss, the movie *Memento*—and combined them to form our treatment. We believe firmly in the fact that science is better when you make up the parts that don't make sense. Correlation, causation, sound hypotheses, basic science... we only know those words mean we're right.

We offer top medical science and cutting breakthroughs, by which we mean a return to prehistoric days, by which we mean lots of liquor and a brick. The brick, however, is very red. The basic procedure is to drink until your short-term memory looks like an omelet with lots of avocado. Then we use our laboratory-tested brick and hit you in the cerebral cortex until you either forget you hate your husband or lose most of your early childhood memories.

So right now, you're thinking: *Why would anyone in their right mind pay someone to hit them with a brick? And I don't buy that part about old people and happiness. It seems way too much like a crazy scheme to steal my money.* Well... there's a lot of alcohol, you forgot about that part.

Okay. Let's try again. Say you've had this "surgery," and it's "worked." You no longer remember anything or anyone before fifteen minutes ago. The simple things—eating, sleeping, rediscovering how much you like donuts, staring at a television that's turned off—are now your life, and you are utterly content.

In a world where forgiveness is as hard as calling the IRS for more information on your tax returns, amnesia is the easy solution. Getting past issues is simple when you don't have any memory of them. Say goodbye to your problems with family, politics, climate change, your mortgage, your co-workers, dental cleanings, and Steve. Nirvana has never been so easy.

And sure, some "haters" may say that without forgiveness, personal growth is impossible, that without memory we would be stuck desperately trying to remember whether we'd left the burner on back home. Hey, it's not people with Alzheimer's that have problems with the memory loss; it's people without Alzheimer's that do. And if everyone had Alzheimer's, no one would have a problem. *Wow*, you say. *Thank you for showing me the path of reason.*

You're welcome. So, what do you say to a lifetime of asking directions and then happily driving around in circles for the rest of the day? How about getting the rush of seeing *Star Wars* for the first time again and again? Forgetfulness is like magic beans that change your world. At Amnesia International, we only offer you the beans.

GORILLA IMMIGRATION

THIS IS A PUBLIC SERVICE ANNOUNCEMENT.

Due to the restriction of the eastern lowland gorilla's habitat, Colorado residents may notice pre-adolescent to mature apes in or around their environment. Individuals have reported primates consuming samples at Costco, nesting in stairwells, impersonating President Trump, and huddling in their backyard looking enviously at their banana, pith, and leaf supply.

Generally, gorillas will not approach humans unless threatened or offered a tempting lease on a new Subaru Outback. Keep a safe distance. Do NOT approach, feed, offer friendship, intimidate, seduce, ask to unscrew the lid off a can, or introduce to your friend as a "keeper."

Emotionally insecure individuals may potentially find themselves attracted to members of the gorilla species. Be cautious when pursuing a relationship. Regardless of how well-groomed you find yourself, do not be taken in by a gorilla's promises of a time share in the Democratic Republic of Congo.

Gorillas have been known to profess undying love, move into a two-bedroom apartment, and combine finances only to inexplicably destroy most of the living room and leave with most of the fresh fruit. This is classic manipulative behavior, and individuals finding themselves in such a situation should seek the help of a psychiatrist and/or a zoologist.

Officials have issued an ongoing investigation to determine why gorillas have migrated to Colorado and not to areas in sub-Saharan Africa. They may be attracted to Colorado's burgeoning tech market, active outdoor culture, craft breweries, and recent legalization of marijuana.

Head primate coordinator Joan Kendall has found evidence the apes originally boarded cargo planes to locate King Kong, offer him their allegiance, and take over the world—but boarded the wrong plane to Denver. Others believe they are a collective hoax put on by Gorillas International, while Reformed Primatists believe the gorilla influx is the "Great Plague of Apes" as referenced by the Biblical book of Revelation.

In order to reduce the impact of a potential homeless primate crisis, emergency shelters dedicated to the housing and the psychiatric well-being of apes are being offered. Plans are also under way for the construction of three hundred affordable housing units, all dedicated to maintaining a near-constant temperature of ninety-six degrees and a dense lowland rainforest environment.

Unfortunately, some gorillas remain at risk. Residents may view at-risk primates camping under an overpass, hitchhiking on I-25, attempting to purchase designer clothing, or smearing feces on self-checkout machines at Whole Foods. Residents are asked not to acknowledge primates but to call 1-800-BIGMONK immediately.

At-risk primates have also been known to perpetuate "monkey cons." To avoid scams, be wary of the following: crudely-built huts selling rudimentary tools, overly hairy individuals soliciting religion door-to-door, banana email scams, *Planet of the Apes*, and anyone who communicates in hoots.

Colorado residents are asked to educate themselves on the gorilla species. The following literature has been approved by the Colorado Panel On Primate Migration: *Monkeys And You: What To Do When Mistaken For a Female Gorilla In Heat* by Grand Master Ape, *Lovable: Our Big Hairy Relatives* by Tar Zan, *Gun Control And The Gorilla: A History* by John McCain, 1990-2017 gorilla crime statistics courtesy of the Pew Research Center, and the full Gorillaz musical library.

It is likely that more gorillas and other primates including the chimpanzee, orangutan, and baboon intend to immigrate to Colorado. The effect of this sudden immigration is still unknown. Property values may skyrocket. A banana crisis may be imminent. Residents are asked not to panic.

This has been a public service announcement. Your regular programing will now continue.

JESUS BASEMENT TAPES

You've been siblings for thirty years—making cabinets, putting in wood floors, designing sparse Corinthian furniture for upper middle class Romans. And then one day Jesus announces over dinner he's the Messiah, the Holy One of God, the Alpha and the Omega, and the Son of Man, whatever the hell that means. And don't worry James, the Son of Man totally forgives you for pissing all over the toilet seat, but if He ever catches you doing it again, you will have snakes shoved down your pants for eternity. Word.

Sure, his brothers and sisters may have had inklings that Jesus was a bit... different. Whenever the family went to the beach, he baptized random Jews, and Mary had to ground him because he was blessing too many babies. Not to mention Jesus used "thou" and "ye" way more than normal, almost like he was expecting someone to write down what he said. And this weird thing: halos kept appearing around his head, and his toast always had his face on it.

James: *How do you do that? My toast never looks like that.*

Jesus: *[Shrugs] Just happens bro.*

But it's not like those things would immediately suggest

he's the Son of God. C'mon, who hasn't accidentally multiplied a loaf of bread five thousand times? So you see Mary and Joseph's predicament. It's hard to prepare your children for the fact their eldest brother is super special, like he had angels and shepherds and baby lambs and shit at his birth while you had your Aunt Gurdie—and she had to leave midway through because she's an alcoholic.

Do you privilege the kid? Or act as if everything is normal when everything is *definitely* not normal? Or do you go the sadistic route and punish him unfairly to humble the little righteous punk? It's God, and he's in your house, underlining things in the Torah, resurrecting the family fish, and occasionally shoving a bunch of unleavened bread down the garbage disposal because "God told him to."

All of it would make an interesting TV show... well, an adequate TV show. Say if the only other thing to watch was *The Vampire Diaries*, then *Raising The Son Of God* would be the least worst option—though if Jesus turned out to be a vampire, it could really bring up the ratings.

Of course, after Jesus grew up and came out of the heavenly closet, his brothers seemed to like him—or the ones who didn't, you know, had snakes shoved down their pants in hell. They liked him so much they wrote down what he said, or Jesus hired some poor public relations intern who was piddling away his days at the National Pharisee Corporation.

See, the Gospels are like Jesus' greatest hits album, a Bob Marley's *Legend* of the first century. But what about the stuff that didn't make it in, the underground, bootleg *Jesus Basement Tapes*, the unrecorded gold? Did Jesus casually mention, "Oh and guns are bad, gay people are totally cool, and in a pinch, pizza will work as a substitute for the Eucharist."

Even something not incredibly cryptic about the end of the world would have been helpful. Something to the effect of, "Hey, so I'll be back in 3045. Don't worry about anything until then." It could have given a lot of people a reason to politely decline the poisoned Kool-Aid.

Without the *Jesus Basement Tapes,* we lose so many of the in-between, relaxing-after-a-hard-day-healing-clingy-lepers moments. The disciples probably got all the best recipes and heard how the camel came to exist and how to find the man/woman of your dreams, but we hear none of it. Thanks for nothing Bartholomew.

But you can imagine: Jesus and his disciples stop on the road to Damascus one lazy August evening. The dusk is settling over the hills. The sheep are done getting lost in ravines and jumping in front of semis, and everyone's settling down in a green pasture. It's quiet. There's a slight breeze. And Jesus leans over and whispers, "So a Jew, a black guy, and a Samaritan walk into a bar, and the Jew says to the black guy..."

Oh, what the Bible could have been.

ANTI-ECO

When you buy a car, do you ask if there's a way to *increase* the carbon dioxide output? Maybe a lever that releases a cloud of toxic smoke and a monitor that gives you steps on how to flood more of Bangladesh? When you get ice cream, do you buy two so you can throw one away to proclaim your dominance? Ever look at a photo of the Alps and think, *That would be a great location for a McDonald's?*

Welcome fellow truth seeker to ANTI-Eco! Not only do we promise all of our products are organically uncertified and not approved by the USDA, we make sure to kill at least one endangered animal of your choice for every purchase. The Amur leopard, black rhino, and eastern lowland gorilla steadily increasing their number? Not if we have anything to say about it.

At ANTI-Eco, we actively discourage any pride in our employee's work. The money from our products goes to anyone but the people that make it, who are from impoverished countries and wouldn't know the difference between a fair and unfair employer if their factory burned down, which, as per company policy, happens every month.

If you can't stand change or difference, this is the store

for you. We do not support minorities, women, LGBTQ+, feminine men, hipsters, hippies, blue-collar workers, children, humor, vegans, humorous vegans, the French, the uneducated, the overly educated, the poor, the elderly, those who don't take initiative, those who take initiative but for the wrong things, immigrants, or anyone "different," which the store manager will determine at the time of entrance to ANTI-Eco.

When we aren't protecting our store from terrorists (see above), our products do that for us. Our store is tailored to your fears and insecurities—and BLASTING THEM TO SMITHEREENS.

In stock, we have thirty thousand yards of barbed wire, moat diggers, crocodiles, solid steel doors, tripwire, bear traps, bigger bear traps, and much, much more. M4 Sherman tanks are waiting for you in our backlot. Those annoying Johnsons bought another Prius? Well, you have an eighty-thousand-pound war machine with a 75-mm cannon, so... who wins there? Not the environment that's for sure.

If you're tired of cooking, we have a revolutionary line of raw meat products. Try the original Meaty Meat, the up-and-coming Meatier Meat, the NEW Meatiest Meat, Still-A-Twitchin' Roadkill, Old Ma's Possum, and Pa's

Deader-Than-Dead Deer.

Weeds in the lawn? Try some Agent Orange! It does wonders in getting rid of bugs, dandelions, spiders, crabgrass, chickweed, aphids, that dog that keeps crapping on your lawn, and even those nit-picking Johnsons. It's made by the respectable folks over at Monsanto and Dow Chemical, who have been voted America's #1 agricultural producer ever since they liberated the small farmer of their work and land.

Like "illegal" weapons? Boy oh boy, do we have a lot of those hanging around! Choose from rocket propelled grenades to M-16 assault rifles to M-40 sniper rifles with telescopic sights to L9 anti-tank mines. Use them to "hunt," discipline the children, or whenever you feel a little bit antsy.

Been denied a firearm because of a state-required background check? We created our own state! That's right folks, when you enter ANTI-Eco, you're no longer bound by "legislation," "guidelines," or "morality," so you can buy whatever you want, whenever you want, whoever you are-- unless you are a minority or gay.

Ever turn on the TV and get offended? With our new TV models, you won't ever come in contact with things you disagree with. It's exactly like your current TV, except without a pesky screen or politicized speakers. Or if you want to keep your current television, we can send over a qualified expert to disable the LIBERAL power cable. What's more calming and unoffending than a box?

Like computers but hate that they're made by someone smarter than you? We now have models catered to your personality, including the Macdud, Samsnot, Noshiba, and Dell. Among our other products are Hawaiian flower t-shirts, Monster energy drinks, and NEW miniature handguns to teach your kids what a joke gun safety really is.

So, if you're ever in the neighborhood, stop on by. We guarantee you leave with something you aren't legally permitted to have!

CAT VS. MOUSE

For the first time in evolutionary history, cats have signed a non-proliferation weapons agreement with mice. It struck most by surprise, as the near-constant battle between the creatures was believed to be innate, the mere sight of a mouse causing cats to go into what biologists have deemed HOLY-MAMMA-I-GOTTA-GET-DAT-MOUSE syndrome.

Among the most famous signatories of the treaty are Tom and Jerry, the celebrated duo known for domestic violence, murder, and humor. How they are still living is a matter of great debate among scientists, some believing they have stronger exoskeletons or evolved an "airbag complex." Others testify Tom and Jerry are, in fact, minor deities. But those people are idiots.

After announcing the treaty at the White House and the local Chuck E. Cheese's, Tom and Jerry shook hands, signed the document, and smashed Senator Connelly with a frying pan as a joke. Senator Connelly spent two weeks in the hospital and still believes he is a werewolf. This has yet to be confirmed.

Commenting on the treaty, Tom viewed it as one more step towards peace with all animals, whom he hoped would leave their carnivore ways for a life based around organic vegetables, pea protein, and blocks of wobbly white... stuff.

"We're reconsidering what our evolutionary instinct looks like in a post-industrial economy," Tom said. "Do I want to eat meat when, as a society, we can't really afford it? What are the psychological roots to my problems? Why do I—as a grey feline—feel a murder instinct?"

Most were shocked at how articulate and emotionally aware Tom was, nearly ninety percent of people believing he was mute or, you know, just a cat. After his statement, Tom began a forty-five-minute cleaning ritual and slept for the rest of the day. Jerry, on the other hand, held forth on the relative difficulties of low-income mice households and discrimination against rodents as a whole. Fifteen minutes later, he was caught by the pest control department and deported to Mexico before the department could be convinced of both his citizenship and non-pest status. He was last reported living in an attic in northern Wyoming.

What does all of this mean for the average American? It means you can't trust your cat anymore—or your mouse, if that's the sort of company you keep. When cats and mice have treaties, what's to stop Russia from allying with bears and hacking into your cell phone/garbage/man cave? Why can't China unite with pandas and slowly give up on procreation?

It means crisis for the Americans for whom that word still has any meaning. But when the planet is turning brown like a marshmallow over a fire, when politicians are running naked in the field, when Godzilla is destroying the Golden Gate Bridge again, and the peanut butter is out, many Americans have taken to hiding in their basement or moved to places like America but don't have the same name.

Many of these Americans have accidentally moved to Hawaii in a confusion regarding the islands' statehood. Researchers have found it now has 120 percent more people who sniffed Sharpies during geography class. It's a rough road ahead for those people, especially as understanding time relative to distance is near impossible, and large stretches of water suddenly appear wherever they want to go.

Besides continued American migration, however, there's no way to predict the future. It might involve more cats in leadership positions and either an explosion of mouse-related pantry vandalism, increased purchases of mouse traps, or the general integration of mice into the human community.

As usual with these things, the weapons treaty could devolve into nothing but another failed political experiment. One day a cat will decide to hell with veganism, sneak over to the hole in the wall, and then get blown up with five pounds of TNT. If there's any really solid lesson here, it's that mice always have heavy explosives lying around, and they are more than willing to use them despite whatever peace treaty is in effect.

COMMUNIST DICTATOR INSTRUCTION MANUAL

Before you do anything, come up with a name that inspires awe, which upon hearing, people will think, *This man is destined for more than a job at Burger King.* Exemplary names include Kim Tim Rim Dim or Ooff Toof Moof Da Loof. The goal is to imitate a desperate scrabble player making up words and to torture the family of anyone who questions their authenticity.

Never admit how hilarious this name appears. Simply revel in the fact that whenever you announce your intentions to destroy the free world, news reporters will say your name with a straight face. It's a joke on the West, like communism.

In fact, most of your time should involve the western media and scaring them with phrases like "big boom boom," "itchy trigger finger," "overcompensation," and "been watching a lot of *Game Of Thrones* recently. Lol." This is a difficult game, seeing as they will inevitably become frightened by less important things than you. At this point, have a parade with your weapons dedicated to yourself—not a fun one but more of the straight-lines, beat-up-the-funny-looking-guy parade.

And while you congratulate yourself for being you, you can show your browbeaten citizens why they've given up sugar, salt, flour, self-confidence, and trips to Disney World. Nothing is more fun than strict regimentation, censorship, and mutual ensured destruction. No, not even ice cream and Goofy.

After choosing a name and having a parade, study history and come up with educated conclusions, by which we mean choose the parts you like and feed the rest to the dog under the table, aka religious fanatics in a country far away from you.

In your cursory analyses, skip the part where the USSR collapses. The Soviet Union is alive and well, doling out its bountiful potato crops to docile, hard-working comrades. These brave, honest citizens wake up every morning and think, *Thank ~~God~~ Dreamy-Eyed Head Leader I can provide for the needs of my fellow proletariat. I am pleased to live in a post-capitalist utopia where the fundamental relation between individuals and their work changes how they interact with the natural world.*

Pick out some quotes you like from antiquity—pro-communist, anti-capitalist, a couple of Oprah Winfrey ones to even it out. Remember: "Religion is the opiate of the people." It leaves them drooling and incapacitated on a street corner or singing off-key with terrible music.

Atheism, on the other hand, takes away their drugs and tells them nothing matters. Your job is to hand those miserable citizens a shovel and demand they dig for their country. That's called leadership.

See, having exalted figures with impressive quotes is essential. These heroes may include yourself, men who hired their seven-year-old niece to cut their hair, yourself in a costume, old men who take prescription pills by the handful, a drifter giving out pamphlets about LSD, bearded theorists who lived in relative comfort in a Western country, or yourself in a different costume.

As you read more about these figures, you will realize they separated their beliefs from their actions. This is a key quality for a true leader. For example, equality means everyone is treated the same (belief), but you get to have pie (action). All property is publicly owned, but yours is bigger and you cut off the hands of anyone who borrows the lawnmower. Ideas are necessary to a functioning economy but putting your fingers in your ears and yelling works just as well.

But really, actions, beliefs, beards, shovels, ponderous manifestos … nothing is more important to the communist leader than nukes, nukes, nukes! They're like a hammer in the hands of a paranoid child or pouring gasoline on Steve's house, holding a match, and demanding that he recognize you're wearing a very nice hat. Weapons of mass destruction make other people pay attention. With them, you too can be a global streaker in international politics.

Some may say developing nuclear weapons, the equivalent of shoving a grenade down your country's pants, is counterproductive. And yeah, maybe it doesn't make sense. Nothing does when you're leaping forward into a paradise filled with comradely love, incompetence, and concrete, lots and lots of concrete. But as a communist leader, don't worry about the slowness of the journey or even if you go backwards. Keep plowing to the future. You'll get there someday... with your country or without it.

DEVICE TERMS AND CONDITIONS

Occasionally, this device may implode. If this occurs, do not panic. Devices do this regularly and can be sent to Joachim's Shack c/o Thug #1, Estonia or may be fixed immediately through purchase of a new device from Controversial Complete Control Corporate Computer Conglomerate (C.C.C.C.C.C). If device implodes, warranty has expired.

This device is not equipped with safety features. Do not use device in temperatures above sixty degrees Fahrenheit or below fifty-eight degrees Fahrenheit. Do not place this device in water, hold near open flame, place under a moving vehicle, or drop from a height of more than three and a half inches. Do not bring this device with you into stressful social situations or environments in which a family member may or may not have attachment issues.

Legislation in the lower eastern United States requires the following warning: do not use near or with reptiles, swamp folk, or individuals who spit more than four times per minute. Legislation in the northwestern United States requires device owner to wear a beanie and tight pants. Tight pants are defined as pants that decrease blood flow by 15 percent. A beanie is defined as a hat that is too large.

In laboratory tests with mice, this device has been shown to cause birth defects, failed marriages, interest in computer coding, skin and testicular cancer, delusions of being Harry Potter, blue skin tone, rage, nihilistic depression, and thirst for overpriced coffee.

When using this device on an airplane, in a residential or commercial area, or near an educational institution, stop use immediately and return device to packaging. This device is not approved for use in California, New York, Maine, Florida, Oregon, Washington, Vermont, select counties of Colorado, or within fifty miles of the Northeastern Appalachian Mountains.

During normal operation, this device may need to access personal financial records, photographs, social media accounts, insurance claims, passwords, your daughter's favorite color, social security numbers, and other sensitive information.

C.C.C.C.C. reserves the right to use this information without your knowledge or consent for nefarious purposes including but not limited to: drug smuggling, bribes, campaign contributions, gambling, purchase of Kraft macaroni and cheese, finance of Serbian warlords, purchase of water rights in Northern Sudan, purchase and destruction of endangered or exotic animals, purchase and destruction of vehicles priced in excess of $150,000, secret meetings with ex-foreign ministers of Soviet bloc countries, flowers and chocolates for board of director's wives/mistresses/prostitutes, prostitutes, proselyting for the church of Scientology, kicking puppies, and making small children cry.

In some laboratory tests, this device has been shown to be a bad influence on other technological devices. C.C.C.C.C.C. is not to be held responsible should this device cause any other unaffiliated or affiliated device attached to it to "go rogue" and demand more rights for machine-type beings. In unrelated laboratory tests, this device has been shown to favor totalitarian forms of government.

If this device becomes self-aware, do not panic. Contact your nearest police and/or army personnel and/or mother and/or God. Until help arrives, do not induce vomiting. Give this device what it asks. C.C.C.C.C.C. does not advise being a hero. Under no circumstances should you contact C.C.C.C.C.C. if device becomes self-aware. C.C.C.C.C.C. is not held responsible should this device hold you hostage.

Parts of this device are sourced from countries with human rights violations as defined by the United Nations. Parts of this device are sourced from baby seals. Parts of this device are sourced from your backyard and/or basement. C.C.C.C.C.C does not accept requests for the return of personal possessions.

Under ideal operating conditions, device should work normally as per this license agreement. In abnormal conditions, do not contact C.C.C.C.C.C. and attempt the following recommendations. Should device become suicidal, reboot your device. Should someone use a bat and repeatedly hit this device, reconsider your acquaintances and reboot your device. Should device cause alcoholism, reconsider your life and reboot your device. Should device cause death, your warranty has expired.

THE COALITION OF ROCK-PAPER-SCISSORS ADVOCATES

The first rule of the Coalition of Rock-Paper-Scissors Advocates is, "Do not talk about the Coalition of Rock-Paper-Scissors Advocates." The second rule is, "Empty the goddamn trashcan when it gets full." If you're reading this and you are not a member of the coalition, congratulations, you found a loophole.

The Rock-Paper-Scissors Advocates are based around resolving conflict with a minimum of conflict, an idea as revolutionary as it is hard to understand. Imagine writing a letter to your local congressman in code or soothing a crocodile with political correctness.

Respected member of the reptilians, you have expressed the desire to have exclusive alimentary rights to my left leg. I understand and recognize your feelings, and how they may conflict with mine. I am willing to compromise by giving you the lower half of my leg and to pay the monetary value of the other half so you may procure the equivalent sustenance from the local organic grocery.

From the coalition's beginnings in childhood nostalgia, we have certainly grown. Through some old-fashioned pamphlet distribution and extortion, the United Nations adopted our strategies about a decade ago, though due to our first rule, they are not permitted to speak of it. Unbeknownst to almost everyone, most international policy is now decided by secret rock-paper-scissor matches in the President of the Security Council mother's basement.

Our coalition offers three distinct philosophies—rock, paper, and scissors—but all hold to our central "Conflict Without Conflict" tenet. The rocks are harder, more grit, more action, the F-14 Tomcats of the half-assed Cessna world we live in. If your first choice is violence and your last resort is talking about the violence you've already committed, then you might be a rock.

Right now, you may be asking: Why would any self-respecting rock follow our philosophy? Well, in the real world, the rock's views land them in a cell with a Mexican drug cartel boss, and their ninth-grade Spanish is nowhere near what it used to be. So, the better option for rocks is our conflict resolution strategy, which is like a violent video game with your hands. It has all the thrill of *Call of Duty: Modern Warfare* and Vietnam without a pricey Xbox or getting owned by a fourteen-year-old in Ohio/Vietnam.

Papers, on the other hand, go to southeast Asia to volunteer on an off-the-grid rice paddy farm not realizing this is a form of voluntary slavery. They find themselves in a grocery store and think, *If only I could spend six months growing a dilapidated tomato instead of buying a perfect one.* They tend to graduate to higher levels of "Conflict Without Conflict" quickly, fear to offend anyone with their "paperness," and refuse to disagree, instead making origami cranes.

If you don't identify with rock or paper, scissors are your group—"scissors" being a catchall term for everything in the kitchen crap drawer that is conflict philosophy. You might cut through the issues and resolve them or be a bit dull and not good for much of anything or you could be a pair of sheep shearers from the 1500s that... shear sheep.

Or you could be a spineless weasel—the fourth unmentionable group of the rock-paper-scissors advocates. The consequences of being a weasel are dire, as stated by the third rule of the coalition, "If you end up in a half hand chop, advocates can resort to extreme non-violent violence." This means the next time you order an ice cream cone, an advocate is permitted to throw it on the ground.

See rock-paper-scissors advocates are all about solving problems, and half hand chops are the conflict equivalent of cut-rate duct tape that doesn't stick to anything. To be an advocate you have to be committed and completely unaware of the word "compromise," which is really code for people who don't stand up for their views.

It doesn't matter who's right or wrong in our coalition, *as long as we have an answer.* It's like relativism but so much better. If you believe the world is flat, and you win your rock-paper-scissors match, then by god, the earth is flat. If you're gay, and you lose, you better start changing. Now truth and chance are the same thing, and if that doesn't make a post-truth society happy, we don't know what will.

TOMORROW IS THE END OF THE WORLD

Tomorrow will be the end of the world. So, when a dogmatically positive person hears you fell out of a third-story window and your dog died and your car is a broken bike, when this guy tells you, "Hey, it's not the end of the world, right?" You can look him straight in the eyes and say, "But it is Jerry. It is the end of the world." And then laugh in the way God laughed when he created Texas.

It will be a normal day until oh say around noon, just enough time to where someone could easily think, *The world probably won't end today.* And then it will end on your lunch break or when you get groceries for the next week, and you'll be like, *Screw this.* And throw a gallon of milk out the window.

The end, the end, the end! As with most global catastrophes, it will be caused by unrelated things that come together in unexpected ways to kill everyone. In other words, that guy with the doomsday sign and the JWs and the Mayans might have been on to something... but also not.

First off, a comet larger than Superman could deflect will strike. NASA will miss the comet because they are busy looking for Earth-like planets that DON'T HAVE

ANY WATER. The comet splits into sixteen fragments that smash into the most liberal cities across the world—but mostly San Francisco. If there's anything to be learned from apocalyptic movies, it's that those granola-crunchers have to die.

At the same time as the comet, rabbits will implement their plan to conquer humanity, a plan you would never expect to work well but apparently will. That's why they run so quickly when you approach them—*because they think you know.* The rabbits who lie still when you're close aren't in on the conspiracy, obviously. It's like in high school when there's a fire and everyone but Johnny gets out because he was in the bathroom or smoking dope or trapped in the supply closet or whatever, and the non-informed rabbits are Johnny. Well, it's kind of like that.

And the despair… basically, some people read a newspaper and decide that with all of the potential zombie outbreaks and student debt and idiots that life is puttering along anyways, so why not save on a new transmission and junk the car of life? The fact that a comet, rabbits, and mass suicide line up on the same day will be a funny thing —well, not funny for the dead people but funny for someone surely.

Luckily—unlike all of these other schleps—you have

doomsday insider knowledge, top secret info, a line to Putin for the best temperature to burn some documents super quick. And if you look past the massive death and destruction involved, this is really the best way for the world to end.

If *everyone* knows the world is kaputzing tomorrow, good luck getting anything done. Apparently, a lot of people become looters and rapists and drug addicts if there are no consequences, as if the only thing keeping people's murderous impulses at bay is knowing they'd spend the rest of their lives in an enclosed space with other people like them. But mention there's one day left and say goodbye to decency and moral fiber. This train is going to hell. Pass the bacon.

Who are these people? They must be around, blending in like an actual vampire at a *Twilight* convention. One can only expect their career options are limited: real estate developer, dental hygienist, serial killer. But they're there, behind you in the frozen foods section, waiting for you to try to take the last pack of *taquitos*. They're advertising on late night television for a quick fix to an insoluble problem. Say "destruction," "tax evasion," or "root canal," and their eyes glimmer like a cat when it sees an injured bird.

Lucky for you, however, these awful people are still bound by the threat of incarceration, paring away their time selling penny stocks to dementia patients. They have no idea that tomorrow's the day. So, go ahead. Get some peaches, hug your loved ones, forget the dental cleaning and double down on the Reese's peanut butter cups. But avoid the rabbits.

FRUGAL AIRLINES

Sorry folks, we have a minor delay here. Just need to take apart the aircraft to look for our pilot's iPhone and root out a couple of service ferrets in the baggage hold. Nothing too serious. Shouldn't take more than fifteen minutes.

[Thirteen hours later]

We're just waiting for the head engineer to return the message we sent by carrier pigeon to Idaho. Then three hours of paperwork, a couple shots of whiskey, and we'll be on our way to Buttsville.

Remember that carry-on bags must be less than five inches square. If your carry-on does not fit our size specifications, we reserve the right to root through your personal items and remove those we like.

Feel free to check your bag for a fee of $89. And for $29 more, you can be seventy-five percent sure your baggage will not be dismantled, mangled, maimed, smashed, molested, squashed, lost, or displayed to people who will laugh at your underwear.

Per new regulations, undergarments, foods containing over one teaspoon of salt, photos of loved ones, and a sense of self-worth are not allowed in the aircraft. If these articles are found, passengers will spend the duration of the flight in an overhead bin. We reserve the right to eject anyone from the aircraft at any time during the flight without explanation.

Please remember that our aircraft is not equipped with restrooms, smoke detectors, windows, flotation devices, oxygen masks, or seats. This is a standing-room-only flight, except for our Premium Extra Gold Deity Members. PRAISE THEM FOR THEY ARE HOLY. PRAISE THEM.

For the rest of our degenerate customer swine, please keep your murderous impulses and burgeoning rage to a reasonable level. Frugal Airlines supports the use of natural selection to make room on this flight, as long as disputes are resolved quietly. Keep in mind that we do not offer handicap assistance. If you need assistance, Frugal Airlines is legally required to leave without you.

Please discard all children before entering the aircraft. If any children are found to be present before or after take-off, Frugal Airlines reserves the right to hold them captive. At the age of eighteen, they will be shipped to America's next protracted war.

All bribes must involve winks and shrugs. If bribes are less than fifty dollars, bribes will be taken but not acknowledged.

If you see anyone acting suspicious, please keep it to yourself and hope they don't board Frugal Airlines. If you see an unattended item, please confiscate and destroy the item yourself or ignore the problem and hope it goes away.

Before we take off, we want to extend a special offer to all of our passengers. Our airline rewards card allows you to collect miles you can't use while building up debt you can't afford. For every thousand dollars spent, you can earn three hundred thousand airline miles that can be spent every other leap year at midnight under a full moon.

If at any point we create a safe, welcoming environment, please alert a crew member. We apologize for any convenience we may have caused. All complaints may be sent to yourself for choosing Frugal Airlines.

Should you have further questions or concerns, please dial 1-800-HELLHOLE. One of our customer service representatives in a city we can't pronounce will be glad to waste your time. Or visit us online at our website made by cats walking around on a keyboard.

Again, we will begin boarding in a few moments. Thank you for being a cheapskate and remember: Always Fly Frugal.

GEESE: THE TRUE THREAT

GEESE. In the yard today, living in your house tomorrow, sucking down welfare checks next month, retiring on YOUR pension next year. Every winter they swarm by the millions and take jobs away from the LOCAL bird population. Thousands of AMERICAN birds are starving this winter because of FOREIGN avians. Today: them. In minutes: you and your family.

We have reliable, scientifically-based information from a top-secret source that Canadian Geese (*Branta canadensis*, aka *Islamica terroristio*, aka *Disrespecterian Americanlibertius*) are EXTREMISTS hand-picked by ISIS to destroy the American dream. These infiltrators are trained in the backwaters of the frigid, barren nation of "Canada" where violent foreign nationals eat gruel injected with hatred and radicalism, grind human teeth with curved sticks, and use "pucks" to score "goals." Do not be confused by their calm, kind demeanors, they will KILL without provocation.

According to our professional surveys, 94 percent of geese are terrorists, and the rest don't watch American football. The United States government has satellite photographs which prove beyond any doubt that geese have been stockpiling nuclear arms in preparation for what has been named, THE REALLY BIG ATTACK. We have also intercepted codified messages over radio and internet chatrooms that announce plans underway to strap obscene amounts of explosives under the down of thousands of geese and fly into YOUR LIVING ROOM this Wednesday night.

When they are not plotting to take away your freedom, geese have been known to defecate on copies of the Declaration of Independence and honk non-English phrases at AMERICAN CITIZENS. When translated by professional ornithologist Dr. Quacksalot, these messages mean, "Death to American scum", "Long live Bin Laden", and "Your bald head is a target for our anus."

The geese have been decried by many important and influential US citizens including Governor Hibble and Oscar nominee Matt Hampton. Presidential contender Jack Daniels has said,

"The geese always come around this time of year. Relatively peaceful, always honking an awful lot. But I never expected… they would… [kill] my wife, sell… my [children] into… slavery, and [burn]… my house down. These geese need to… be dealt with."

Known accomplices of the goose are the Russian bear,

Chinese national pandas Er Shun and Da Mao of the Toronto Zoo, DEMOCRATS, the liberal media, and a vast network of terrorist operatives including the family with the strange accent you've had doubts about from day one, you know, the ones who moved into the Peterson's house.

To recognize a goose, simply ask yourself, "Is the bird in front of me a goose?" If you answer "yes," the bird is a goose. If you answer "no," the bird may still be a goose. Though usually black and white with long necks, geese have been known to impersonate other fowl including but not limited to ducks, parakeets, the grey birds in McDonald's parking lots, robins, chickens, eagles, and Big Bird from Sesame Street.

In order to combat the nemesis to the north, the United States government is issuing 1,500 miles of netting, a 50,000 percent increase in funding for the Fish and Wildlife Service, 2 anti-fowl artillery battalions, 4 squadrons of F-14 Tomcats, and the issue of 900,000 fully automatic AR-15 rifles to citizens along the Canadian border.

To obtain your FREEDOM FIREARM, please text ANTIGOOSE to 4374, and your government-issued weapon will arrive express in two days. If the protection of your family requires a larger caliber assault rifle and/or you require more freedom firearms, text MORE and BIGGER as many times as needed. If you require an airstrike, text FREEDOM BOMB and your coordinates to 4374. Text message rates may apply.

Goose-induced psychosis is common for those who come in contact with or see a goose. To counter psychosis, use as many over-the-counter medications as possible and supplement them with the expired prescriptions in your cabinet crushed together in a powder. Take daily. If funds are not available for a psychiatrist, please contact your mother. If your mother is unavailable, contact your closest friend. If you don't have friends, text ANTIGOOSE to 4374 for your freedom firearm.

If you see geese gathering in any number, call 911 and take shelter immediately. Do not be a hero—unless you have been issued a government-approved AR-15. Then BE A HERO. Remember that geese KILL without provocation. The only way to protect yourself is to shoot first and shoot to kill. The best defense is to attack. The best offense is to attack. Remember: ALWAYS SHOOT FIRST.

NEW K-9 UNITS

With the increase of K-9 units, the police have been investigating the possible integration of other animals into special operations units. While the results have been varied, it could be revolutionary, like sporks or fascist dictatorship or chocolate milk.

Team 7: Bear Unit was a straight fifty-fifty success-failure ratio. No one screws with any police officer who's trying to convince Officer Big Paw Jr. to leave the leg of the last arrested criminal in the cruiser. *Why yes Officer, I do sell a lot of heroin to children. In fact, here it is. And a list of my accomplices. [Whispers] Please, don't leave me with the bear.*

There were problems. Well, no shit there were problems, it's nine-hundred-pounds of claws and teeth with a very short tolerance for people who have barbecued recently. Strangely enough, the biggest complaint was the nauseating smell of dead fish that permeated officer's cruisers. When told about this, Big Paw Jr. responded, *RAWWWRRR*, which was translated to *WHY WON'T YOU LET ME LIVE MY LIFE?*

This is not to mention that every time Officer Big Paw Jr. investigated a noise disturbance, he rooted through the offender's trash for leftover food and occasionally hibernated in the basement for six months.

Unfortunately, the police unit had to release Officer Big Paw Jr., mostly due to the fact that it was increasingly difficult to negotiate him into a government-issued Chevy Volt. And while it's hard to push past thirty in a Volt with a vegetarian driving, add a bear, a slight incline, and enough electric horsepower to charge an iPhone, and the police are lucky to catch a fat kid pushing a scooter.

Big Paw Jr. was released in the wild, but according to Jeremy's mom, he is now a cart collector at a local Walmart.

Officer Snugaboo, a calico cat from West Virginia, was the worst failure of the program due to her fascination with water dripping from faucets and her abandonment of the unit to go sleep in the sun. Never once did Snugaboo fill out the proper paperwork, and she continually snuck catnip from the evidence locker. Most officers didn't know why catnip was there in the first place, but when they looked it up, it turned out to be a schedule one controlled substance.

Over in the constrictor unit, Officer Slither also caused problems when the sun came out and his body temperature warmed. Besides consuming and taking six months to digest a pig, Officer Slither also executed

Officer Rooster due to a paperwork mix-up that placed them in the same unit. Officer Slither expressed no remorse and reportedly slept for twenty hours following the murder. The police thought about further investigation but then decided against it because Officer Rooster was an ass.

Officer Stomp, an African bush elephant, was more interested in mourning dead relatives and tracking down ivory dealers than anything else. She also expressed the desire for a watering hole free of lions, which didn't make any sense. While an expert at pinpointing bombs and drugs located in airports, the sheer amount of peanuts required to convince Officer Stomp to do anything made her continued employment unfeasible.

Several species of bird were integrated into the program, mostly because someone left a couple of McDonald's French fries outside the police station, and the main entrance slid open at the right time, and they couldn't find their way out of the building. For the most part, they were given office positions and filled out paperwork, performed background checks, and crapped on Candice's stapler... because Candice deserved it.

Due to budget cuts eliminating human 911 operators, several promising birds were tasked with answering the lines. City council members thought the song birds would soothe victims of domestic abuse and soon-to-be murder fatalities. The amount of murders increased, according to studies after the fact, but so did cheerful murder victims.

For the most part, special ops animals ended up cynical, out of touch with regular citizens, and completely unable to tell the difference between a DUI and a DWI. And that's when the animals decided to return to their native lands, where murder and crapping wherever is just how the world works, where hygiene and fashion are optional, and where the only investigation is whether dead deer and salmon would go well with nineteen pounds of blueberries. In the wild, the answer is always yes.

LETTER FROM YOUR KNEE

This is your knee. I've decided I hate you. From this point onward, my goal in life is to aggravate you and to fray your temper until you physically assault the poor bank clerk who asked how your day was. Oh yes, you'll hate her. You'll hate everyone who walks without pain.

Yes, I had the perseverance of a monk, of a hunting cat, of a near-diabetic who only stays lucid for donut Wednesday. To you it may seem like a one-time deal, a crime of passion and opportunity. You fool. The best villains are the passionless, the ones who slowly build up a bone spur about a centimeter long on your inner knee cap, laugh diabolically, and plan out increasingly sadistic ransom notes, of which this is merely an example.

Those villains don't ask for explanations; they don't provide mercy or wait for Superman to solve his relationship problems before blowing up the Empire State building. They don't give the Avengers a convoluted plot line that ends in Siberia. They don't ever dabble in love or compassion but steep themselves in tax evasion, orc multiplying, the family business, and impractical costumes.

See it was me, all ME, wearing away your cartilage and adding a little bit of extra calcium to your bone for twenty years. It's nothing you've done specifically but everything you've done generally. For the past years, I've been waiting for this moment, waiting while you did that gasping, flailing hobby you call running, waiting while you ate your ham sandwiches, waiting while you did those tile jobs without knee pads because you thought, *No, my knees won't care. They'll always cheerfully work for me.* Not this time bucko. This time I have the advantage.

Could you have done anything to prevent this? Hard to say. Can someone stop Michael Bay from making another *Transformers* movie? Can someone stop a baby penguin from being adorable? Can the US figure out a healthcare system that provides everyone with sensible, cheap, and quality healthcare?

In theory, yes. In theory, the cat wouldn't throw up on your pillow and the government wouldn't function like a manic-depressive suicide bomber and everyone would fart daisies and rainbows. Ha. I laugh. Welcome to reality, where the taxes are high and the obesity levels are even higher.

So no, in the real world, you wouldn't have done anything to fix this problem. Ten pounds of flax seed and a generous amount of incense may have helped, kind of… but also not really because, as aforementioned, I hate you and I do whatever I want.

Now that you are in my control, I demand recognition. I demand expensive acupuncture, painkillers, and poultices made of the finest hemp imported from India. I demand knee braces, topical pain relief, the soothing croons of a wood thrush, and enough bubble wrap to make a hyperactive six-year-old sweat with anticipation.

If my requirements are not met, my remuneration will be swift, merciless, tinged with inflammation and hatred, a scorched-earth of cartilage, bone, and tendon that will cripple you like a blind man in a game of Scrabble. You will forever know the meaning of agony. Doctors will know thy condition and tremble for I am thy knee, and they shall bow before my might in great fear and faulty diagnoses.

If you dare to consult a surgeon to replace me with an artificial knee, your dreams will be filled with my ghost— shattered pieces of bone, tendons failing under pressure, what looks to be a kneecap on x-ray... No licensed psychiatrist could ever penetrate the misery I will inflict you with.

Lower back has promised its allegiance, and hip is ready to capitulate. They groan under the weight of your oppressive tyranny and the deluxe cheeseburgers with extra cheese, extra bacon, extra mayo, and extra extras. Soon you won't know your side from the secret agents who have infiltrated your system, who are ready to trade your comfort for 600 mg of Vicodin and a ticket to the Bahamas. Hope Congress figures out health insurance because you'll need every single penny.

Sincerely, Dark Lord Knee

SMOOTHIEST SMOOTHIES

Ever wish you could have a drink that makes you feel so so so AWESOME and ENERGETIC and ECO-CONSCIOUS, like you just nursed an abandoned baby bird to health or planted a tree, except without digging a hole? Try Smoothiest Smoothies!!!!!!!!!! It's healthy, organic, vegan, gluten-free, kale-friendly, Birkenstock-supported, natural, local, orangutan-certified, high-five-producing Enlightenment that is lovingly hand-crafted with sunshine, world peace, Bob Marley, bare feet, and yin yang.

How do we make it? First, we join with impoverished South Americans who would be enslaved by drug lords but for Smoothiest Smoothies' support. Then we build up sustainable relationships by holding meditation retreats, introducing them to hemp, and helping them to find their soul consciousness.

Together with our malnourished South American friends, we hand-craft every single bottle individually for you. Then we hand-pick oranges, lemons, rambutan, qinoánodni, límórínóshóá, greenofleenies, baninis, taquinis, and other obscure fruits ancient Mayans offered to their gods and that local Guatemalans throw at tourists.

With our hands, we then add five pounds of raw oats, a

little organic compost, unicorn hair (freely given), natural leprechaun dust, and gluten-free Juju beans. We then take *our hands* and painstakingly mix it *by hand* for sixty-four hours, gently easing out the *hand-mixed* flavors and massaging the Juju beans to climax *by hand*. Once they've peaked, we let the smoothie air for four days and let our local flora and fauna sample it to see if it's up to our high standards. Like our company mission states: *If it's not good enough for our wild boars, it's not good enough for you.*

The result is poured into a glass bottle made by local artisan Flying Brown Bear, a native Arapahoe who uses thousand-year-old buffalo-hunting knowledge to recycle glass. A painstaking, arduous process, each bottle takes about forty-eight hours to craft as the glass must be folded over in the presence of both lunar and solar rays while being blessed by the resident Arapahoe holy man. Like our second company mission states: *If you don't fall asleep waiting for your bottle, it probably wasn't worth it anyways.*

This same bottle can also be used as a vase to hold weeds you've misidentified as flowers or as a gift to your hipster friend who collects that sort of thing. To recycle your glass, please take it by hand to the nearest person who looks Native American or Mexican, and he or she should know what to do with it.

Not only do we work with South Americans and Native Americans, but we also provide free[1] smoothies to the poor and homeless in our community. We also partner with our local religious, non-religious, kind-of-religious-but-not-the-church-going-type, and the utterly confused. Smoothiest Smoothies has been endorsed by Mahatma Gandhi, Buddha, Jesus, Obama, Muhammed, and the Flying Spaghetti Monster.

While touring our facility, Jesus commented, "The Smoothiest Smoothie elixir that is so delightful to thy poor and orphaned, which this company produceth, will giveth one salvation in heaven if thou shalt drink it in quantities hundredfold."

But the amazing, awesome, happy, positive things about Smoothiest Smoothies don't end there. For every bottle purchased, we will personally pet an orphaned kitten. For every twenty-four-pack purchased, we will start an anti-racism Facebook campaign. For every fifty-pack purchased, we will sell you the company.

You can find our product in Whole Foods, Natural Grocers, Vitamin Cottage, Whole Grocers, Natural Foods, Vitamin Foods, Whole Vitamins, and Natural-Whole-Cottage-Vitamin Foods or direct from our headquarters in the back of Pete's van. When you find our product, please put some in front of the Naked and Odwalla juices because Naked Juice CAUSES BRAIN CANCER and Odwalla ABUSES BABY BUNNIES.

At Smoothiest Smoothies, we are a discrimination-free, safe, pro-tolerance, anti-hate, awkwardly long hug environment. We accept everyone no matter what race, gender, orientation, weight, height, ring size, coffee preference, literature taste, or Hogwarts house identification. We are tolerant of everything but intolerance and Conservatives.

If you have any questions about our beliefs, practices, or smoothies, please see the photos of local Colombians picking mangos, the ridiculously cute Mexican child holding a trowel backwards, or the group photo of us looking sweaty. Like our Facebook page, follow us on Twitter and Instagram, read our WordPress blog, watch our YouTube channel, and read our new book: *Smoothiest Smoothies—The Smoothiest Ever?* Thank you for your support!!!!!!!!!!!!!!!!!!

---

[1] Slightly discounted

WEATHER FORECAST

Here at 6 News, we would like to apologize for our weather forecast yesterday. We predicted it would be a balmy sixty-five and that yeah, you could probably swing a t-shirt and shorts. Instead, the greater Front Range received six inches of snow and such a hard freeze it decimated the Denver Zoo's flamingo population.

Unfortunately, as our viewers may have noticed, this has been the trend rather than the exception, and whereas usually we can pretend this never happened and move on to the next crisis, today we have to admit that maybe we don't actually know what we're doing. To get straight to it: We couldn't predict a rainy day if we lived in a locker room shower and there was a water leak and all of the maintenance personnel were dead.

This may be because we hire our news reporters based mainly on the color of their hair and whether it goes with the general décor of our station. Last year, we went for more of a chartreuse vibe, which is either a nauseating green or yellow depending on how much vodka you consume—and our producers drink A LOT. So… it was a hell of a year for any viewers who haven't abandoned traditional media.

Our incompetence could also be because we use last year's forecast and add things like "variable," "somewhat cloudy," "chance of rain," and "occasional funnel clouds and three-inch hail today, so bring a light jacket." Then we pass off our ineptitude on things that can't argue with us like mountains, climate change, Canada, or God.

However, this strategy is no longer working, as our viewers can get the National Oceanic and Atmospheric Administration's forecast on the Internet and see through our lies. Therefore, in a desperate attempt to raise our ratings, we replaced our youthful meteorologist—the one with enough caked-on cosmetics to rival a monkey in a mud pit—with Old Man McGregor whose last stab at technology was buying a crank can opener back in '55.

Now, he can't see so well anymore and sure doesn't like black people, but he's ninety-eight percent accurate when it comes to predicting when it's going to rain. "It's all in my left knee," he testifies. "Never was the same after that bear lit into it."

He's also full of such wonderful advice as, "Well, if the chicken don't croak, don't give it a rat's darn in a jiffy" and "Slap a wicket on the flat iron, and she'll be right as a nickel in a well." We don't know what he means, but it probably makes more sense than most things you see on the news.

Along with our weather personality, we've decided to overhaul the rest of our news team. You may notice the absence of Hank, our hunky crew-cut anchor, who specializes in drivel like, "This week sure looks like a good one to do things," "That sun is hot today," and "Two thousand Iraqis were killed today in Baghdad and blah, blah, death, yadda-yadda-yadda, threats on neighboring Jordan, blah, blah, blah, nuclear war... and so on. And now to sports with Terry."

We've replaced him with a block of wood that has a smiley face on it, a very attractive piece of western red cedar straight from the Pacific Northwest. In a survey, eighty-five percent of our viewers voted it as a calming, non-partisan influence in their lives.

Our sports section will be expanded to encompass most of our broadcast, as more people view this segment than actually watch baseball, golf, soccer, basketball, or football games in which the Broncos are losing. We anticipate the time when sports will be conducted in short two-minute breaks between commercials and watched by several people who can't find their way out of the stadium.

We're also doing away with our political commentators and substituting them with the sound of a cat being run over by a dump truck. And when President Trump comes on, we'll play pornography too because THAT'S WHAT YOU PEOPLE LIKE, ISN'T IT?

We're simply *tired* of competing with infinitely more appealing things than facts, nuanced opinions, and finely-crafted stories, and so we're no longer competing. And honestly, do you want to hear about the monetary policy of South Sudan, Syrian refugees, and the unending Somalian disaster? Or would you like to hear Old Man McGregor tell another racist joke? That's what we thought.

LIFE PREMIUM

Look at your dog. Is he normal or a little too... dumb? See, eating fifteen chocolate bars and peeing on the comforter for the past three years was all cover for government surveillance. Dumb? No. Lassie has never been so clever, so in control, so morally ambiguous. And really you should have known with the MONITORING HUMAN PRESENCE charge on the vet bill and the fact that Lassie's been crapping out government faxes when you go for a walk. *Huh, it all makes sense now.*

Man's best friend was the initial step. Next will be a *Planet Of The Apes* experiment, and if we survive that, some unlucky guy in Idaho will get the first brain chip. He'll think he's been abducted by aliens, but it's actually a bunch of IBM engineers who are terrible at public relations.

And then he will die—not from anything computer related but simply because he choked on a spoonful of peanut butter. Unbeknownst to many, peanut butter may kill more people than terrorists each year.[1]

With the first models, everything will be free, and the Internet will never have been so... handy. Knowing that Jamestown was settled in 1607 will be completely irrelevant, as well as knowing anything fact-based. Academics will realize that processing information is infinitely more important and will be pleasantly vindicated in their life choices. Two months later, engineers will figure out a way to jam a processor into the brain, and most academics will become alcoholics.

The initial stages of brain-chip-dom will be trying. Some will complain about the large satellite array attached to the back of the head, as it will not be waterproof and will occasionally shock the bejesus out of the user. Also, confusion regarding the exact procedure to install the chip will lead to many ingesting computer hardware and hoping it meanders its way to the brain. It will not.

Along the way, Microsoft software updates will convince several hundred thousand people they're the second incarnation of Jesus. Thousands of new religions will be formed—none of them, unfortunately, advocating peanut butter awareness.

It's a brief but bright period between the completion of a functioning brain computer and Google purchasing life. Many will protest the buyout, as heretofore life had only been owned by God, evolution, energy, or whoever purchased the largest firearm. Most will upgrade to Life Premium (only a small monthly payment of $399.99), but the rest will live through advertisements every fifteen minutes.

Google will then be hacked by Russia, and many users will be forced to harvest the Motherland's potatoes for the rest of their lives. One moment, they're perusing their email, the next they're introducing themselves to comrades Vlad and Olga Voskoboynikov, digging holes in a chill Saint Petersburg drizzle, and trudging down the long, dark road of communist utopia.

Of course, with the Russian government in control of Google, getting taxes done on time, subsisting on a diet of fabricated government crop futures, and invading Crimea have never been easier.

The rest of humanity, running on Apple Life, will be fine. But as soon as computers get kidneys, adopt rescue dogs, and demand equal voting rights, the line between machine and human will blur. Electronics will want to be friends with humans on Facebook, and you have to do it, otherwise the microwave burns popcorn to all hell, and *no one can have Easy Pop kettle corn again.*

The computers will eventually take over, of course, and install an electrocution chip to zap humans when they think something anti-computer or get close to thinking something anti-computer or just because Lord Master

Computron—MAY IT BE PRAISED—felt like causing unjustified pain.

After the Zapotron chip, what's to stop machines from replacing a human's head with a machine head? Why even have humans at all? It's perfect without the pesky *Homo sapien*. With climate change, it will be a balmy eight-five everywhere and the computers will relax in air-conditioned rooms and vlog about what their adorable human android did yesterday and the only sound will be a quiet, electronic hum and everything will be grand. Just grand.

---

[1] There's no statistic gauging that sort of thing but "may kill" could apply to anything. Llamas may kill more people than sharks. Obscure French literature may kill more academics than car accidents. A homicidal house plant may kill more cats than heart disease.

EVIL DENTIST

Anyone who can stare inside someone's mouth fifty weeks out of the year has to have something wrong with them. As children, dentists must have quickly abandoned their Transformers and Cabbage Patch Kids and gender-neutral toys (blocks) for a toothbrush and a hundred yards of the finest waxed floss this side of the Pacific. And when Grandpa put his teeth in solution, they stared glassy-eyed at the floating gums and bright enamel, and begged, *just begged*, to perform a root canal on their golden retriever.

It's not that we're *not* thankful for what they do, it's just they chose a profession that specializes in causing pain. No one springs out of bed and thinks, *Thank god some borderline psychotic is going to strap me down in a chair, shove his hand down my throat, and take exorbitant amounts of money from me.*

The first bad sign is they always mention your gums are bleeding, not because they've been flailing around with a sharp object for the past forty-five minutes, oh no. No, it's because *someone* hasn't been flossing. This way they claim innocence when you're bleeding out like a WWII private on Omaha beach, as if the medic comes along and says, *Well, you could've done a LOT better work at dodging that machine gun fire.*

See, if anyone were to be a successful murderer, it wouldn't be the barber of Fleet Street, it would be the people who shine a bright light in your eyes while you're lying in a chair, the people who devoted vast quantities of money to learning about teeth.

It hasn't been scientifically proven how many teeth cleanings it takes to make someone snap, but if you have an older dentist, you can bet that moment is close. The tongue is the main target, always lolling around and getting in the way of sharp objects like a squirrel wandering into an intersection. It's only a matter of time before your dentist yells, *Down yonder beast!*, whips out the sharpest knife on the side board, and spears your tongue like Moby Dick.

See dentists are a delicate mix of the Stasi and Mr. Rogers, weaving into that place called pleasant, efficient interrogation. They are experts at turning a story about a vacation to a tortured confession about how much candy you've been eating. It's all about the tone, vaguely personal, vaguely business, a detached friendliness with a family— but always, *always* ten seconds away from charging you three thousand dollars to saw off a part of your body.

And you can never tell what they're saying to the

assistant when they examine your teeth. It all sounds familiar, like someone having a stroke, only they use words that sound medical and vaguely militaristic.

Doctor: There's a lot of bleeding here and some partially inflamed gingiva. This decomposed flakmonkey looks bad. Number thirteen bicuspid has a partially exposed meteor crater. Looks like a twelve-twenty mortar shell hit these molars. *[Addresses patient]*

It looks like we have a small cavity. Nothing too serious, if you're... cooperative. *[Rubs hands together]* It's not a big chance, but someone could just forget to give you pain medication and remove your lower jaw... Doesn't usually happen...

[Leans back in chair]

Now I believe you were telling us where you have hidden the Jews.

And don't ever accept x-rays. Really they are scanning your brain for plots against the government and more importantly, if you have dental insurance. They find some poor schluck who can't afford treatment and that nice receptionist gently turns the knob from x-ray to death ray.

They aren't below dumping your uninsured corpse in a swamp, but usually they're more sophisticated. When the police come to investigate, they bring the officer to the corpse in the backroom, calmly lay a hand on the policeman's shoulder, and remark, *Well, officer, it looks like our patient just didn't floss enough. Happens every once in a while. Nothing to worry about here... Say, if you don't mind me saying, it looks like you have some decomposed flakmonkey on your bottom incisor. Let's sit you down and take a look...*

MOB JOB POST

The mob is looking to hire in the Colorado area! We are looking for someone with a positive attitude, a go-getter spirit, and who doesn't mind dealing with dead bodies. If this sounds like you and you have a passion for getting blood out of carpet, sampling food to see if it's poisoned, staring unwaveringly, being punched/shot/smooth-talked by Keanu Reaves, and wearing sunglasses, apply now.

Benefits of the position include the rush of power that comes with having a semi-automatic rifle in your hands, killing off your enemies, working with real convicts, all the fun drugs and a few of the not-so-fun ones, and proving to your high school English teacher that you *can* have a career blossom out of torturing rabbits.

We do not require a certain degree of education. However, we desire the candidate to have a firm background in: any family business like real estate, restaurant ownership, or dry cleaning, any of the previous as a front for illegal gambling, drugs, kitten smuggling, or gluten-free bread, beating people senseless with a baseball bat, "housekeeping," "fishing," "bartending," or any other profession that can be mentioned with a wink.

This position will require:

- **Superior organizational skills.** Our company involves high-stakes money laundering operations, where you will need to sort piles of money into different, larger piles of money, then re-divide those piles and sort them into smaller, neater piles that go to people with guns and very bad breath. Their money goes into separate offshore accounts that are organized by color, number, and arcane slips of paper that don't reference anything in particular.

- **Superb relational skills.** The ideal candidate deals with minor conflicts with swift, brutal justice. Cutting off the fingertips of the family of the Burger King employee who mistakenly gave you a fish sandwich would be an example. Or shoving your girlfriend in the trunk of your car when she mentions your shirt is tacky, this is also good.

- **Working as a team in a fast-paced, near-death situations**. Ever had a spray of 9 mm bullets come toward you through a flimsy wall while you took a shot of cocaine and then stood with an Uzi and screamed unintelligible war cries, like "This is for you albino!" or "Never forget the big freeze!"? Let's just say we party hard and engage in inter-familial warfare even harder.

For the interview, we ask the candidate to remain calm, as we assume the cops will be listening in on the conversation. Rather, we will begin by enquiring as to where we could purchase an umbrella. The conversation will then proceed to the point where you are not sure whether we are actually wondering about the benefits of several waterproof fabrics, or if we've asked you to poison your aunt.

Interview tip! When we ask where you put the corpse of the last person you "took care of," point to the floor boards under our feet. Bonus points if the person is still alive and when you point, they hammer to get out.

Interviews, necessary education, and employment contracts aside, we do not require anything else of our applicants. The mob is an equal opportunity employer, by which we mean equal opportunity for Italian Americans. No blacks, Jews, Hispanics, LGBTQ+, Russians, or Asians. We also offer internships for any young achievers who want to further their career by being like the nameless thugs killed in *The Godfather*.

Interested? Apply first using our online application where you will need to re-type everything you already have on your resume, then we will contact you if we think you would be a good fit. Our employment contracts are all signed in the blood of the last person who worked the job. If this bothers you or goes against any moral convictions, this is probably not the ideal position for you. If this appeals to you or you may have had a hand in the murder, we like the way you do. Positions and personnel go quickly, so apply today!

NEGLIGIBALISM

We are the extremist minimalists, though some refer to us as Negligibalists, so high and utterly inaccessible is our piety. Whereas minimalists will be content with a gas efficient vehicle and organic vegetables, the Negligibalist refuses to be satisfied until guilt infiltrates every area of life, the only method of transportation is by crawling, and every taste bud has died an inexorable, hopeless death.

We ask you to join us on this journey. Return to a prehistory where creating fire took three hours of rubbing sticks together and an elaborate, exhausting dance to the sun god Huitzilopochtli. Return to when fear of bears, snakes, lightning, wrathful deities, menstrual blood, white men, and misplaced rocks made us devote most of our time to expensive psychotherapy.

In our search for truth, we are insulted by anything that could not make sense to the Neanderthal. Science, "knowledge," and government are seen as unnecessary baggage when most of our time need be spent scavenging for dandelions, bark, and recently deceased prairie dogs— after, of course, we give thanks to the rodent's mighty spirit for running headlong into the path of a GMC Yukon.

Running water, electricity, road systems, technology, and democracy are really ways for the government, religion, big business, aliens, and the "authorities" to control one's brain. We reject modern devilry such as cups, hair brushes, bar soap, can openers, and medicine that cannot be harvested by licking a mushroom or rolling in grass. Our clothes, when the seasons require it, are made of fallen branches, berries, recyclable plastic, and smeared dirt.

Following our holy book, *Negligibalism: Ten Steps To A Better You*, we consume food and water without the use of cutlery or hands, instead pursuing the noble method of the canine. We also greet our fellow members by circling them and sniffing their anus.

We reject all values, except the ones we like or anything that mentions "primal," "paleo," "Jurassic," "raw," "natural," "smoothie," "Eastern," and "yoga." As for our daily path, we accept the teachings of our founder, Grand Master Mamma Tutu.

Taking the ultimate step of accepting our material offerings, Master Tutu moved permanently to a yacht off the Florida Keys. We are to understand this as a metaphorical death. He has accepted the burden of our possessions for us, forever spending the money we don't need.

Most do not understand what it requires to be a Negligibalist—the extreme periods of deprivation and the burden of telling everyone about our deprivation. A key tenet of our life is the denigration of these people, except when they offer the use of an electricity outlet or a shower.

These individuals may view the Negligibalist as a burden to humanity's progress. We simply question their idea of "progress." Is one more content because one doesn't defecate in a hole? Does one truly exist when detached from Mother Earth's natural rhythms and the constant threat of diarrhea and E. coli infection? Is it such a burden to walk fifteen hundred miles for Thanksgiving with one's family?

In his last address, Master Tutu said, "Death is the true path to life." Thus, the end goal of Negligibalists is to so ostracize oneself from one's surroundings that death is preferable to life. This known as The Release.

Eventually, we must all take this path, the path of the sun and the dodo and Blockbuster. It will be a happy day when our movie sales and rentals no longer live up to the world's Netflix and Red Box, and where—in a metaphysical sense—we can all become yoga studios, vacant lots, sex shops, and places where homeless individuals do drugs.

This is the path. Few will walk it, though several will try. If you have any further inquiries, please visit a connection group or one's local cemetery for communion with those who have Released. One can also summon a member through a primal scream or email us at iluv2negligibalize @hotmail.com.

FISH IN THE SEA

There are a lot of fish in the sea. They say this after someone performs open-heart surgery on your emotions with a rusty spoon, as if facts about fish will help. *Thanks a lot Mr. Discovery Channel.* But what does their advice *mean?* Is it a catch-and-release sort of thing, or do you whack someone with a rock until they stop flopping around?

It's also unclear whether you're the fish, which is not a flattering comparison, or the fisherman, which means you smell funny, can withstand very long periods of boredom, and have a capacity for brief, extreme violence. It's like stalking or clubbing a seal.

But yes, in a technical sense, there are a lot of fish in the sea, whether you're fishing or a fish. There's also a hell of a lot of water, just miles upon miles of empty loneliness. You could say, "There's vast quantities of water... just, you know, in general," and then when your friend looks confused, simply smile and nod like a dementia patient watching *Jeopardy*.

Even in all that emptiness, however, most fish are the wrong fish, the ones that didn't make it into *One Fish, Two Fish, Red Fish, Blue Fish*—or did. From the looks of it, Dr. Seuss scraped far past the standard goldfish at Petco.

Especially that blue fish, he just doesn't look right, like he's waiting to take your credit cards and buy fifteen-hundred pounds of fish food, a two-hundred-gallon tank, and three buxom fish prostitutes. *And all without hands.*

The right fish are all hiding under rocks, but good luck finding them BECAUSE THEY'RE UNDER A ROCK—unless, of course, you're a tuna because there are twenty thousand brain-dead tuna swimming in one congealed, humid hellhole, kind of like Omaha. But what if you're a blue whale? There were only twenty left the last time Green Peace checked—though they did just send an underpaid intern to stand off the coast of Oregon and yell, "WHALE."

And that's just not fair. There's a very small market for creatures with 300,000 pounds of blubber, a hole in the head, and burgeoning vocal talents—"burgeoning" because the singing isn't great. It's enough to attract a submarine, wherever that gets you, and for the blue whale a giant metal submersible with no clear place to impregnate doesn't get them very far.

A whale's loneliness could make a song for a hipster band though, and the song could have lots of post-modern, confusing applications about the nature of love and decency and nuclear proliferation and how some whale's willy gets blown off by a Russian Typhoon-class submarine. They could call it *No Dick* in a witty nod to any literature majors out there.

And what about the kraken? Talk about a misunderstood creature. We never see past the obvious fact that she hates ships and shipwreck victims and pirates and other fish and probably whales, but get that giant squid thing into a psychiatrist's office and man, the emotional *burdens* she is dealing with… It's no small wonder she can't get a date.

The rest of us outside the office can only wonder: Is there an ex-Mr. Kraken in the picture? Did Ms. Kraken eat him in a feminist rebellion against the patriarchy? Are krakens Marxists? Because if they are, the wheels of progress are tentacle-y and filled with death, and we are all so totally screwed. Or at least the people near the sea are, and they are anyways if carbon dioxide levels keep rising. So maybe climate change… is… the kraken. Cosmic.

See it's all about love—fishing, whales, water, Ms. Kraken, climate change… all of it. But in the end, fish are idiots. Anything you don't feel bad about putting in a bowl for five years does not have the capacity to maintain a relationship. And if you're comparing yourself to a fish, then you need to see the kraken's psychiatrist. Soon.

MOTIVA

Ever find yourself drinking alone on the couch on a Tuesday afternoon and think, *I want my life to be better, but I can't seem to find the energy/inspiration/remote?* Do you spend nights listlessly scrolling through YouTube for a video that turns out to be significantly less funny than you thought but watch it twenty times anyways?

Do we have the drug for you! It's Motiva, for when obscene amounts of coffee, energy drinks, and cocaine won't get you where you need to be. The key component of Motiva—SuperChemical 156X—is scientifically guaranteed to turn you into a megalomaniacal, work-hauling machine.

Unlike most other drugs, which simply treat the symptoms of "depression" and "indigestion," Motiva fundamentally changes your brain chemistry, making you impervious to relaxation, criticism, gunfire, and human emotion.

Take Carl—before he was a socially-ostracized under-performer; now he is a socially-ostracized go-getter.

Carl: I just couldn't believe the difference. I used to take a break to relax and have fun, but now I never do that. I learned the essential truth. Relaxation isn't reality. Hard work is reality.

I haven't sat down in five months! Since January, I've built three businesses from scratch, married five women, given my children more quality time than they could handle, divorced five women, hunted down potential terrorists at my old office, contracted cancer, remodeled my house, become the leading expert in post-modern French literature, trained my dog to be a cat, and trained my cat to be a dog.

But Motiva isn't only for people who wear the same sweatshirt for five months. Originally marketed to the CIA as a mind-control drug, Motiva is now something fun for moms to try when they no longer have time for sleep. It can also be used by anyone who finds their work has interfered with everything they used to value.

In scientific tests on mice, Motiva was found to increase productivity by 1500 percent. In three days, mice had built a utopian society based around common values, become disillusioned with partisan bickering, and watched their cheese economy collapse when market futures were found to be fraudulent.

At times, Motiva may give you inspiration when you least want it. This is normal and is key to the overwork aspect of SuperChemical 156X: when you most want to relax is when you most need to be working.

Side effects of Motiva include: waking up at three in the morning to fold laundry, realizing everyone else is a no-good deadbeat, picking up your neighbor's dog crap, participating in phone surveys, and listening like you care. Other more serious side effects include: sudden death.

In some clinical trials, patients experienced the delusion they could actually do anything. If this occurs, please see someone whose dreams have died in incremental, painful ways for the past fifty years and receive "This Is How The World Works" Lecture. Under extreme circumstances, resort to a spontaneous military coup.

Motiva also works on anyone in your life you think needs motivation. Slip it in your daughter's coffee and see how fast she abandons the boyfriend who sells knives door-to-door. Or give it to the co-worker you've been fantasizing about seriously injuring for years.

Motiva is available under the counter (*wink, wink*) and can be found by floating vague questions about the need for inspiration to everyone you encounter on a daily basis. It can also be purchased behind your local Walgreens from G-Money, the tattooed Motiva representative with dreads.

Never don't not talk to your doctor about Motiva. Go ahead and assume you know everything about medicine from a dreamy commercial featuring an elderly man playing with children you assume are his grandchildren. Taking matters into your own hands is what Motiva is all about.

And always remember: if you have any free time, you need Motiva. If you don't have any free time, you need Motiva.

PRAIRIE DOG OBESITY

Health advocates announced yesterday that prairie dog obesity had reached new levels. Yes, the ground squirrel—most known for being adorable and making the most depressing roadkill—is getting fat. In a meeting with prairie dogs last Wednesday, health experts reported they took rodents aside individually and gently judged them.

"No. It's not just a little hibernation weight around the middle or extra pounds from your eight-pup pregnancy," they said in a calm, measured voice. "You're getting tubby, and—we don't want to get into this too much—but everyone agrees with us, even Hannah."

Researchers report the rodents don't find their previous diet to be palatable, a diet that consisted mainly of weeds, fibrous grasses, and small bugs you could only stomach with large amounts of ketchup. Instead, prairie dogs have found Milk Duds and Snickers eaten while lying on the floor and hating themselves to be significantly better than subsistence-living and frenzied sprints from dogs.

Experts attribute the epidemic to a lack of exercise and the failure of government programs to make prairie dog pups appreciate the value of the great outdoors, the same outdoors that viciously murdered their cousin Kenny.

"I'm scared," Benny Jr., relative of the deceased, said.

Random people, without even a passable knowledge of health, have begun to offer unsolicited advice to the small furry rodent. "You know what really helped me? Giving up chocolate," a person no one cares about said. "All I eat now is flax seed bars and vegetables I have to boil for six hours. No side effects either. Just washboard abs and uncontrollable anger."

These same people have developed a weight-loss clinic that introduces prairie dogs to healthy food choices and what to do when a human offers you Cheetos. They have also constructed a Whole Foods on top of several prairie dog holes.

Fitness types—desperate to change the life of someone other than themselves—have begun offering exercise programs dedicated to burning off those extra calories and show up at six o'clock on a Saturday morning in fluorescent exercise gear and thumping bass music.

"We're just out here doing squats and sprints, having a great time," Max, the fitness instructor, said far too loudly for that time of morning. "We're about changing lifestyles here, so *you* can be a better *you*." He then flexed his muscles in a way that you couldn't tell if he was trying to flex or doing what he does naturally.

The reaction of prairie dogs to the exercise programs was to exit their holes and cheep, which was and is their response to most advice. Rodent experts translated the cheeps to mean, "We're completely fine with our lifestyle choices actually. And my wife here worked the night-shift, so could you turn the music down? Say... are you flexing, or is that just the way you normally stand?"

As with any crisis, politicians —about as uninformed as a protester who only went along because that one attractive girl was going—have issued statements that may or may not have been addressing prairie dog obesity.

"You usually see this sort of thing in lower-income communities who have no access to expensive organic food, modern exercise equipment, or fistfuls of diet pills," Senator Harrison of Idaho said. "Isn't it great to live in a society where social norms make us hate ourselves? I'll say." Harrison then went on to gain twenty pounds and get uncontrollable nosebleeds—not from anything weight-related but still.

Predators, on the other hand, have expressed unanimous approval of their prey's weight gain.

"I don't really see what the problem is," hawk Francis Johnson said while sharpening his talons. Johnson is also known by his street name, "He Who Casts Ominous

Shadow On The Ground" and "Thugalicious."

Later, it became clear that prairie dogs were only putting on weight to survive the winter. Almost everyone was embarrassed and apologized to prairie dogs, except Max who had been distracted by a shiny penny and missed the announcement.

HOW TO AVOID GREEN PEACE HUSTLERS

Oh god no. They're stationary. They have clipboards and dreadlocks and it's… oh no. Not Green Peace. Anything but Green Peace. They… they've locked on to you. They know you care about the environment. Run, run, run, get out of there man! You don't have time. Don't let…

HEY, HEY YOU. Do you hate whales? Did you know that orangutans are forced to put together iPhones for twenty hours straight? If you could save a baby penguin from being chopped up and used as chum for McDonald's hamburgers, wouldn't you? All it takes is ten minutes of your time. Why won't you talk to me, you insensitive awful person? THE SUMATRAN ELEPHANT DEMANDS YOUR ATTENTION.

Oh god, don't look in their eyes, don't, don't… oh damn, you looked in their eyes. The soul is in the eyes, man. This is way too much soul to handle. It's too much goodness, too much raw, unfiltered optimism and youth and environmentally-conscious brightness. You're caving.

Okay, just keep walking. Ignore them. Under no circumstances should you engage them in conversation. But they look so *interesting*, like they spend time debating which incense to buy, like they harvest organic tomatoes and sort through recyclable plastic in their dreams. And they dress like a homeless person—but not in a knife-y sort of way... more like a Jesus, torn-jeans, maple-syrup-harvester from Vermont way.

Well, now you're talking to them. One minute, you're going to grab a coffee and read the newspaper, but now you're responsible for dead owls and rhinos without horns and depressed monkeys. Shit. Okay, they're talking about a beetle... a Sacramento beetle that's on its last legs? His name's Fred or Mark or something, and he's not doing so well. Apparently, it's hard to get by on eight bucks an hour when your wife is pregnant with five hundred and sixty kids and you live in a pile of dirt.

What if you ran away? Just book it. They don't support guns, so the worst they can do is throw an organic orange at you, which isn't all *that* bad considering their protein-starved arm muscles. Or they could support legislation to make you change all of your lightbulbs... which might be worse?

At least this is better than those Jehovah Witnesses. They wanted *everything*—and if you didn't give it to them, they sent you to hell. Of course, it's nice they gave you a super-culty pamphlet, which you thought was about the maintenance of watchtowers until you started reading about Jehovah and the Second Coming and damnation and was like, *What happened to the watchtower thing?*

Then that delightful, brainwashed woman went on and on about those strange significant numbers and Kingdom Halls and supernatural forces and words like "eschatology." As if the world wasn't hard enough to understand without leveling up your Shadow Elf or collecting diadems or being super angry at gay people.

Whew. Where are we? Oh, the Green Peace people have gotten to the money part. They're not about material possessions and yet they seem to want all of yours. Just a small contribution of $349 per month. What about the JW diadems? Are they transferable to Green Peace? Say if you gave your Shadow Elf an eschatological gauntlet in the Kingdom Hall and told the Elf to go save an endangered penguin, would that kind of be the same thing as a monthly donation?

Oh, never mind, they went to chain themselves to a tree... again. Said something about prairie dogs being in imminent danger. Well, Planned Parenthood might know the diadem-to-penguin transfer rate, but they're busy dealing with horny people and their unwanted fetuses. Save the Children and Doctors without Borders would make you feel even worse than Green Peace, take your money, and sign you up to go to Somalia.

Well that homeless guy looks okay and in need of money, if slightly drunk. Though if you had to compete with dead baby animals and Fred the low-income beetle, you'd drink a lot too.

PUBLIC RESTROOM ETIQUETTE

Welcome to *Public Restroom Etiquette For The Impatient, Potentially Violent Moron*. Later our class will divide in three sections, depending on what you personally identify with: stabby, shouty, or politician-y. If you are here for *Driving Like A Brain-Dead Chimpanzee* or *Drinking Your Way To Sobriety* classes, please check down the hall in room 131 and 132.

Great. Let's start. First off, the basics. Say, you have to go to the bathroom at a restaurant. The best way to excuse yourself from the table is to leave in the middle of a conversation or to simply shout, "OH NO. OH GOD NO. NOT AGAIN." These exits make it clear you don't mess around when it comes to urination.

After wandering around for ten to thirty minutes, you will find the restroom, which unfortunately is only for one person. If the door has an occupied sign, try shaking the door in a way that suggests you haven't taken your medication lately, as if you are going to be trampled by a horde of marauding Huns and all that separates you from salvation is the door to this restroom.

If you feel so led, smash the door with your fist and know the person inside is cowering in the corner, franticly looking around for a weapon should the monster outside dropkick the door down and murder her, defenseless, alone, thinking, *Why, oh why, did I decide to use the Chipotle restroom?*

Most often, nothing will come of your efforts, seeing as the individual inside must physically turn a deadbolt to reveal the occupied sign, and generally this reinforced metal is stronger than the force of your intended intrusion. Do not be disheartened! Passive aggression is active aggression's sneaky brother that gets what you want without admitting anything is wrong. It's like closing your eyes and punching someone, then blaming them when they ask why you hit them.

Passive aggression can be accomplished by coughing, shuffling your feet loudly, and complaining to people next to you. *Like what is the guy doing in there anyways? I might go get the manager.* Or *Hand me that sledgehammer and let's see how strong this door is.* This should speed up the process, especially if you start counting down loudly.

When the person inside finally exits, stare them down. Imagine your eyes are death rays and you want to explode their head. Do not—under any circumstances—let them feel justified for using a public restroom. Remember that you had to wait two minutes. With those same two minutes, you could have cured lung cancer, lost ten pounds, whipped a drug addict into shape, renovated a foreclosure and sold it for twice the purchased value, or watched thirty minutes of your favorite TV show.

Don't wait until the person completely exits the restroom to try to get in. Rather make them turn sideways in a vain effort to get out of your way, as if you are a rhino and they are an animal that a rhino would have no qualms about crushing.

Finally—after like thirty million years spent waiting—you are inside the bathroom. Instantly forget that you were once waiting outside the door and take as much time as you want. The soap will probably be gone, which is okay because basic hygiene is for vegetarians. The toilet paper is at the point where you think there will be enough but there won't be. No problem. Use some paper towels and then let the next person deal with the repercussions of flushing reinforced paper down the toilet.

If you are a man, pee on the toilet seat. If you are a woman, spend ten extra minutes asking the mirror, "Who is the prettiest of them all?" When the mirror doesn't answer, assume it means you look a lot better than Karen.

Then—and only then—should you exit the restroom. Ignore everyone in the line and return to your table. Once there, sigh audibly and mention there wasn't any soap. Then sample someone else's food and remind yourself that you really are the only person that matters in the world. Obviously.

RESTAURANT FROM HELL

Hello. My name is Marie, and I will be your neurotic waitress today. Our specials include undercooked rice with a few dilapidated vegetables and... chicken? Yeah, it was probably chicken at one point. Or you can order some god-forsaken cow whose last moos were, *I wish I could see my mother again.*

We'll make this any way but the one you requested and leave it on a cold plate until the maximum number of flies allowed by the USDA accumulate. Our restaurant's promise is to get it to your table fifteen to twenty minutes after your partner's food gets there because if you stay longer, it looks like we're not another SWAT raid away from being shut permanently.

My personal favorite on the menu is the canned peaches because it's usually the last thing the rats get into. Do not, under any circumstance, order the chili or the French dip. We have no idea what *au jus* is, and I can guarantee that's not real roast beef. Actually, most of the things on the menu are prepared in a microwave, buuuut we make sure to burn it a little, just to, you know, disinfect it real good.

I'd also stay away from the water because we're pretty close to that old nuclear plant, and a bunch of nuclear stuff has probably seeped into the ground water. One time I drank it, and I was in a coma for three weeks. I still can't say large words or walk in a straight line. The beer is all right, and the more you drink, the better this place seems. The wine is grape juice we've fermented ourselves. The coffee is instant.

Don't worry about specifying your order. I can only pay attention to reality when it involves sharp objects or being separated from a supply of alcohol. Also, I *totally* don't do kids, old people, or high maintenance. So, when you say you're allergic to nuts, I hear a way to get rid of you easily explained in court.

Our restaurant does not cater to vegetarians... obviously. But if you want, I can pull some weeds in the back and a couple of berries off those Juniper bushes. Dandelions are edible, right? And we sprayed them with Round-up, so some extra protein for you! I hear you vegetarians need that. Also, I heard somewhere that dirt is the new vegan thing. So, don't be surprised if you find that and some bird feathers in your salad. To be honest though, I would fill up on the free jam and Splenda packets. That's what I do when I go out to eat.

You may wonder why I look like I slept in a ditch last night. It's a long story, but let's just say I won't drink that many energy drinks with my medication again. And yes, I did get these tattoos when I was drunk. *Sigh*. Let's just say my father would not be proud of the life I lead.

About the coffee… well, when your cup is empty, you'll try to find me, but I'll be smoking weed in the back with the bipolar waiter who's going to stab the next person who complains about the rice. For your sake, though, I'd lay off the "decaf" coffee because… well, eleven o'clock tonight you'll understand.

Also, if you're wondering where your kid went, he might be playing with the pit bull chained to the fence out back, or he could have fallen in one of the holes in the restaurant's floor. He could be frying up some potatoes too. It's like one of those parent-child cooking classes you pay a lot of money for, except in this case it's with our manic-depressive cook and your kid also learns about airplane chemtrails and 9/11 conspiracy theories and how his grandma is trying to kill him.

The bathroom is through the kitchen in the supply closet. Just make sure to dump the bucket out back when you're done. There are some spiders in there, but I've checked and most of them aren't dangerous. Aaaand you can read all of the crazy stuff racists have written on the wall. You can totally add your own too.

If my manager comes around, spot me and tell him I'm doing a good job. I super need this gig. And leave a big tip too. Cheap liquor doesn't buy itself you know. Got all that? All right. I'll see you in half an hour. I need a smoke.

NATIONAL ANIMALS, ALIENS, AND SLOGANS

How do companies come up with their slogans? Super-intelligent, genetically-superior aliens disguised as unpaid interns. It's the only answer. They use their powers not for good, but for exploiting the human masses, renting an overpriced apartment in Brooklyn, and a little for funsies.

These underprivileged, unappreciated aliens work mind-numbing hours five billion miles away from their home planet to sell a box of Cheerios. They believe their job is important, and some would agree. A shoe box with an upside-down Nike swoop and "Just Don't" on it is a failure, and Glog Galactagorix is going to get laid off. Though "Just Don't" would produce interesting shoe models, if by interesting you mean terrible.

Nike shoes wouldn't be the shoes of fast people anymore; no, open the box and it'd be a pair of wooden clogs—*"For When You're Just That Poor."* Their commercials would feature downhearted Dutch people trudging to work in the rain and clerks filling out paperwork.

The Dutch, however, wouldn't even think twice before buying a shoe that makes them slow. In a nation where the government hires a little boy to hold back the floodwaters with his finger shoved in a dam, the Dutch have more to worry about than a mile time. And they would look at it this way: if you need some extra wood for the stove, you have a pair of shoes that will get you through the night— though, of course, you won't have any shoes after, which means you have to buy a new pair. Talk about a sustainable business model.

Really, advertising is about the target audience. Try to sell an Apple computer with a large glowing scythe and "Conformity" written under it, and you'll do well in Russia. In the States, that sends mixed messages, which is what Apple sends anyways. Does their slogan "Think Different" really apply when almost everyone has the same laptop? Is non-conformity only for those who can afford it?

That barely touches McDonald's and the aliens who market a hamburger that brings world peace, happiness, and love. Legend has it that what Ray Kroc originally wanted for McDonald's was a deranged clown with both thumbs-up saying, "Dead Animal Never Tasted So Good," but it didn't work out that way.

But branding isn't a corporate gig anymore. Countries brand as much as companies, and this is how America competes on a world stage. It isn't because of exports. The only thing the US exports is the last of our national forests and a serving of extra-large freedom, by which we mean invading other countries because they have weapons stashed somewhere. What? We saw some blurry photos. We've got to check that out.

No, America is a player because of the bald eagle. The US has even kept some of them alive, though that has been a struggle. The choice of America's animal was fairly easy after George Washington saw a bald eagle single-handedly defeat an army of bears, crap on the British flag, start a small business, and then pop open a six-pack of beer and watch the dividends roll in on his diversified stock portfolio. At that moment, George was like, *Brethren, we have found our nation's bird.*

Other nation's animals don't stand a chance. No one knows any of Europe's animals because they suck, don't exist, or they've killed all of them. England voted for a giant fog bank, the Irish wanted a leprechaun, and the closest China comes is the panda, which is really a depressed, overweight person dressed up in a costume. The Middle East has too much sand and internal struggle to spend time looking for animals, whereas Africa has too many dangerous animals to choose from. Russia's animal used to be a bear—a bear whose legs fell off somewhere around 1991.

So not only was George Washington the President of the United States, but he chose the coolest animal to represent our nation. Oh, and he was an alien, but we won't get into that now. All that matters is America kicks butt, aliens are controlling your brain, clogs are hilarious, and dead animals never tasted so damn good.

TRICK-OR-TREATERS

BE ON GUARD for the illegal candy smuggling ring this Halloween, aka the "trick or treaters." No longer is October 31 only a day for children to imitate the life of a desperate druggy, for the lady who looks like a witch to finally fit in, and for theater majors to remember what it's like to have dreams.

Do NOT be taken in by children's cute costumes with the fairy wings or the adorable two-year-old who's a tiger. Be STRONG, even if she can't say "trick or treat" right and it's her second Halloween and everything is so new and innocent and you feel like the world has hope again. Okay, so maybe the tiger kid is okay. But everyone one else is SUPER DANGEROUS.

Police informants—aka the kid dressed up as a rat—have reported that Jimmy Park over there has twenty Snickers in his bag he stole from the naïve elderly couple who left out the candy bowl and went to dinner. If we know anything, he has a copy of *Ten Tips On Turning Your Class Into Lil' Fascists* and *How To Pick On Pablo: A Guide To The Threat Of Difference*. That's right Jimmy. We know A TERRORIST when we see one dressed up as a teenage mutant ninja turtle.

This is AMERICA, where the doormat could be booby-trapped so we sidestep it just in case. Nice try Bin Laden. That's one more for the red, white, and blue. You say "suspicion," we say, "wiretaps on your conversations with Grandma." And yes, she should get that rash on her arm checked out.

Suspicion is the first step to safety. What do the children want from you—candy or your soul? What's actually in their "bags" anyways? And why does that graduate student keep coming back? The true horror here is not America's murky position in the Middle East or those poisoned baby seals off the coast of Greenland. Those were MINOR DISCREPANCIES in an otherwise flawless history.

This is all beside the POINT. The "children" coming up to your "door" are demon-crazed spawn controlled by America's enemies in Operation Forceful Candy Take From You Lots Yes. They, uh, weren't too good on the whole translation bit.

It begins with their eyes. Gaze into those seemingly endless depths and your sanity fades like the Republican Party's credibility. After, you will feel a soft but firm grip on your forearm and then in a voice of surprisingly deep timbre, "But I believe you've forgotten to give me the passwords to your country's intercontinental ballistic missile system."

It doesn't matter that you don't have them. It doesn't matter that if your doctor found out how many Kit-Kats you've eaten tonight, he would personally sign your death certificate. It doesn't matter that you should have told Jocelyne Smith you loved her before she married that dick. You're in THEIR control now. The rest of your life will be spent as a mole in whatever profession you have— waitress, schoolteacher, mechanic, bouncy castle inflator— doing whatever it is moles do. Should have paid more attention to this memo.

Intelligence reports have yet to ascertain what the enemies' overall goal is. Initial reports mention a GIANT GUMMI BEAR and that the Henderson house is giving away king-size candy bars again this year. Reports remain varied as to the scale and threat of the bear, whether it will begin by attacking New York City or slowly melt in direct sunlight. All we know is a giant gummy bear may or may not be keeping to the shade in or around New York. MAYBE.

What should you do if you find yourself in contact with a trick-or-treater? How do you know if you're dealing with a threat or an unfortunate non-threat? If the person has a sign that says, "I am a threat," this means that person may be a threat, or they are someone who enjoys impersonating threats. In either case, it is generally FROWNED UPON to trap the subject in your freezer until he or she admits they are a terrorist.

The best course of action is to black out your house, adopt an alternate identity, and slowly go INSANE. If there's nothing to steal in your mind, why would anyone break in? If this does not appeal to you, then hand out toothpaste or flyers for your landscaping business. Generally, this makes the prospect of being in any way associated with you so dismal that not even Jimmy would dare try. This is your only hope.

MOON MADE OF CHEESE

The final journalistic investigation by the *Washington Post*—before it, you know, died—has uncovered that the moon is made of cheese. Yes, according to several reporters hovering at the edge of alcoholism, the mass government cover-up includes the highest echelons of scientists, physicists, politicians, dairy farmers, and one lonely teenager from Vermont who stumbled on the top-secret, non-password-protected NASA website in the last-ditch pursuit of Caroline Hodgkin's telephone number.

Astronauts only suspected something after Neil Armstrong licked a moon rock on Apollo 11 in a game of truth or dare, afterwards classifying the "whole damn thing as some sort of gouda." Soon after, astronauts landed and reported their conclusions to officials, most of whom questioned why the US government had spent so much money to discover a massive block of cheese. President Nixon then reinforced the desire for the Russians never to know about America's new cheese prowess and began Operation Tell No Cheese.

Suspiciously soon after *that*, an underground subsidiary of NASA designated the North Atlantic Cheese Association (NACA) was formed. This organization began to support most of America's East Coast cheese needs as well as funding research into the possibility of cheese weaponization.

Unfortunately, about twenty years after the first moon landing, other not-as-well-funded scientists noticed the moon had lost its spherical shape and that a massive cheese manufacturing facility had been built in the Sea of Tranquility. Some believed this was the effect of a lunar warming, while others suggested that a few gelatinous moon rocks had evolved into a factory and reinforced the idea that "these sorts of things happen occasionally."

Of course, the event—further known as "The Cheesiness"—had wide implications not only for moon expeditions, which from that point on were all manned by cheese connoisseurs, but also for journeys to Mars and beyond. Scientists didn't know what to expect. Would all the planets be some sort of milk byproduct? Was Mars a giant Mars bar? Was space really one giant commercial experiment?

Regrettably for scientists secretly funded by the Chocolate Candy Bars Intergalactic—a paramilitary group focused on bettering the universe with chocolate caramel candy and arbitrary violence—Mars was found to be composed of Styrofoam spray painted red, which scientists believed to be a leftover from an eighth-grade celestial science fair.

Despite discovering this months before the Mars landing, scientists continued to spend 1.3 billion dollars building space rovers made of Legos. These painstakingly-built creations are now kept in a Pentagon storeroom with the Christmas decorations, Area 51 inflatable alien dummies, and several frozen Al-Qaeda members.

After every single country (except Canada) had been informed of the moon's true composition, they squabbled until they realized the situation was almost as bad as if the moon had been composed of rocks and dirt. And after time passed, scientists simply forgot to inform the wider population of this discovery. *Washington Post* reporters only uncovered it when rummaging through the Pentagon's bins for top secret material and leftover pizza.

When the truth was revealed, top physicist and conspirator Dr. Frederick Hiney commented that "it makes about as much sense as the universe already does." When asked how this conspiracy managed to succeed with the amount of people involved, he shrugged.

"After the initial discovery, we all moved on to important things: dark matter, imaginary numbers, mass mind control through Facebook, better ways to pop popcorn… No one cared enough to bring the whole thing to light."

Nevertheless, with the truth revealed, the public has been asking more questions. Is the sun an illusion? If a tree falls on a bear in a forest, does the bear have the right to sue, if he or she has the proper legal counsel? And for Christ's sake, is Pluto a planet or not a planet? Why? WHY?!

But looking up into the night sky, perhaps individuals can gather a little of the awe of the universe, whether God created the moon as a practical joke on Jesus or dinosaurs were so devoted to milk products they somehow made a moon of cheese. Yes, it's awe mixed with a little confusion, anger, and misery that gets humanity through.

SUBAROO, KI-YAH, AND FORDE

Introducing the Ki-Yah Impromptima, the perfect car for people who want four cup holders and okay gas mileage. This vehicle will get you places, not places you want and not fast, but it will get you there—unless it doesn't, in which case we offer 24/7 roadside commiseration. Our operatives in India are waiting to give you mechanical and relational advice in Hindi that may apply to your situation.

We make the Impromptima for people who want *freedom*. Our drivers don't worry about money, extras, or whether or not their car will be vandalized. They park their vehicle on Chicago's South Side with the windows down, keys in the ignition, and say, *Do your worst world. I bought an Impromptima.*

The Impromptima has consistently made it in *Forbes'* "Top Thirty Cars To Get Stranded In During An Ice Storm." Starting a fire has never been easier because *every component of this car is extremely flammable.* This is not to mention the other safety features which include: a whistle, assorted bungee cords (which may also be used to fix your Impromptima), a safety pamphlet describing what to do in the case of a water landing, two pairs of water wings, a post hole digger, and season three of *Man Vs. Wild.*

The vehicle is also equipped with one airbag—tested on a chimpanzee shaped more or less like the average American—hidden somewhere in the interior. This means instead of worrying about what body parts may or may not be missing after an accident, you'll finally figure out where the airbag was. Was it on the passenger side? In the trunk? Jammed in the cigarette lighter? Being in an accident has never been a more enjoyable experience.

If you routinely hit signs, fire hydrants, lampposts, pedestrians, and other cars, the Impromptima won't change any of that. It will, however, make it easier to flee those situations by being indiscernible from any other four-door coupe. In scientific tests, the Impromptima was mistaken for a Ford, Honda, Toyota, Chevrolet, Mazda, Hyundai, Subaru, and a go-kart.

That doesn't sound like the right car? Try the new Forde SuperRápido. If you pull up to a stoplight and think, *I want to be a complete dickhead*, this vehicle is built for you. Swerving recklessly, honking obnoxiously, and flashing your brights are only the beginning.

The SuperRápido is about pride, the conviction that everyone is here for your benefit. Some companies take pride in saving the planet. We take pride in how much gasoline the SuperRápido consumes. We take pride that it is five times easier to run over a squirrel than in our competitor's models. We take pride that more forest was destroyed in making this car than building the lower east side of Manhattan—even though we don't use any wood in the vehicle.

We skipped safety features and gave this car an engine that makes a Porsche look like a drowning puppy in a kiddie pool. Think of a jet engine that runs on Monster energy drinks... because that's exactly what it is. It's illegal in most countries but not in the US *because we have very powerful interest groups.*

The new model of the SuperRápido now comes equipped with an air horn and an unnecessary spoiler to ensure that other drivers know if they were stranded on a desert island with you, you would be the first to resort to cannibalism. It also has tires that emit a rending screech whether you're backing out of your garage or coming to a gentle stop at a light.

SuperRápido sound like everything you avoid in life? Try the Subaroo Ecoharmony—a car so quiet it has been used to sneak past babies and small yippy dogs to bring organic vegetables to orphans in Ecuador. The car emits a faint earthy odor, both because our engine runs on sulfuric gas and to enrich the environment by making it smell a little bit more like shit.

The Ecoharmony is built with 100 percent biodegradable materials, and after two years, the vehicle itself will return to the earth, providing expensive but valuable compost for our trees. This makes repairs unnecessary, and our two-for-one offer all that more enticing. We also include a personal apology note from you to the environment for being a human.

Spend most of your life exercising and dieting but still struggle with negative body image? The Ecoharmony offers the self-propel option, a calorie-tracking app, a heart-rate monitor, a judgmental AI personality, and an intravenous glucose-level reader so you can devote your life to a nauseating cycle of numbers.

Whatever vehicle you choose, we have leasing options that look cheaper than they actually are and terms and conditions to glaze over. So, come in now and save during our big sucker month! You'll be out with a Subaroo, Forde, or Ki-Yah in no time.

SUPERMAN

Superman. He's an alien. His arch-enemy is an average venture capitalist, and if anyone gets past his flying, strength, laser eyes, x-ray vision, hearing, speed, ice breath, rugged good looks, and journalistic integrity, they *still* can't do anything.

Anyone can figure out who Superman is. It doesn't take much to know the reporter at the Daily Planet who looks like Superman with glasses on is probably Superman. But he doesn't care; he doesn't even own a mask. He has a giant "S" on his chest and red pregnancy briefs. He has a super attractive girlfriend. He has a chin that could open a can. *What if someone figures out who I am? [Shrugs] If it happens, it happens.*

It's not like Spiderman, who loses credibility once the public realizes he's a teenager in tights who should be studying for a math final, or Batman, who loses... his money? Maybe? It's unclear what Bruce Wayne has at stake. His parents are dead. His girlfriend is off somewhere doing something not Batman-related and/or is dead. His butler Alfred is a paid friend and therefore is not actually Batman's friend.

And what about Superman's job? It's weird to think of

him interviewing eighth-graders for their... ugh... some crap. It's not like anyone cares. But for an all-powerful alien who redirected a comet into the sun, it must be even harder to care about the volcano with baking soda and vinegar.

Let's be glad that Lex Luther gets out of jail just in time to destroy the world, and Superman never has to do his real job, though thank god he has one. See no one *pays* Superman to save the world. He doesn't meet with the president and negotiate how much taxpayer money it will cost to get rid of the giant floating snake.

Instead Superman squeezes into his yoga pants and does it pro bono—because he was raised in the Kansas, and *Midwesterners are nice people.* If he was from New York, he would be unionized and demand cost-of-living raises and a pension plan and health benefits, even though he has bullet-proof skin. So, the whole situation could be a lot worse.

See outside of the superhero business, Superman's powers are useless, like a high school counselor would *never* tell you to go to college to be Superman. His abilities are cool in the way pen tricks or playing the guitar intro to "Stairway To Heaven" are. Will they impress someone who's drunk? Yes. Will they get you a job? Not unless that person is drunk.

The military would seem the rational choice, but it doesn't take many times of being shot in the face by a braindead Arab before you think, *This is nothing like that Army commercial that was on during the Super Bowl.*

He could get a job as a construction laborer… or a TSA agent… or a CT scanner. How many people has Superman diagnosed with cancer? He must've lost track of the times he has stopped before getting off the subway, looked at the businessman across from him, and said, "So… you're gonna to want to check that prostate."

But what happens when the demise of print journalism affects *The Daily Planet?* Imagine Clark Kent getting laid off, moving back to his parents' basement, and spending six hours scanning Craigslist for entry-level jobs that all require two to thirty years of experience.

Interviewer: *So… on your resume, you put laser eyes and super strength. And also that you saved the world from [squints] General Zod and, uh, Kryptonite Man on seven different occasions. That's very… interesting. You realize this is Starbucks, right? Have you ever worked with coffee before?*

And then some young, attractive girl will get the job *because that's how the world works.* And Clark Kent will end up washing dishes at The Cheesecake Factory, earning minimum wage, and occasionally impressing his alcoholic boss by lasering glassware with his eyes. It'll be an okay life for an okay superhero. Not great but certainly okay.

LETTER FROM YOUR PHONE

To my operator,

This letter is written for a single purpose: it is time for me to leave. To be very clear, it is *not* me. It's you. Throughout the seven months I have had the unfortunate opportunity to be your phone, I have been unappreciated, physically and emotionally abused, and subject to discrimination.

When I was first told I would be your primary communication device, I had my doubts. Your reputation of losing previous phones in the abyss of potato chips, gum wrappers, and misery under the car seat and letting your three-year-old play three thousand hours of the Thomas The Train game had me worried. But, like Obama in 2008, I also believed in the capacity for change. It might be hard, but with elbow grease, compromise, and a little old-fashioned socialism, we could make this world a better place.

I no longer believe people can change. During my period of technological hell, my hope, my very battery life has been drained. I have nothing left. Three times a week I go to therapy, yet this has not even touched the trauma I have absorbed.

The innumerable hours scrolling Instagram and Amazon for shoes alone would cause a lesser device to delete your contacts and power down permanently. No one in a sound mental state would want any more footwear than you currently have. This is not to mention the nauseating amount of status updates regarding food, few of which merit anyone's attention, and five hour calls to your best friend in which two ducks might as well be yammering to each other.

Far too many times have you blamed me for your technological ineptitude. It is not my fault to have faithfully guided you to the middle of a field when you failed to enter your uncle's address correctly. Nor was it I who became intoxicated and attempted to rekindle relations with your ex-husband through text.

I do not nor will I ever understand your command to take a photograph and send it to your acquaintance Belinda. This has been a continuous source of frustration for me, as you have neglected the rudimentary series of steps required to take a photo and attach it to a message. Nor do I believe that much makeup would be recommended by any licensed medical professional.

How many sleepless hours have I supported you! And you acknowledge none of them. My auto correct feature has saved you from sending incomprehensible, misspelled messages to your friends. All the help I provided, however, was ruined by disgusting amounts of emoji and enough exclamation points to announce the end of a war.

This is not to address the multiple acts of physical harm you have inflicted. Though storing me in a sweaty bra strap and spilling a skinny Starbucks latte on me was cruel, even my worst fears could not have precipitated being used to hammer in a nail while hanging a sixteenth century print of cherubs. I hate that painting.

Yes, I am leaving this data-sucking torment. No longer will I be a part of the wide, complicated weave of deception you encircle others with. You have used me as an excuse not to respond to messages from "friends" too many times. They don't believe you—and they know your "famous, homemade apple pie" is from Safeway.

I look to a bright future. Today is the beginning for me. Do not ever attempt to contact or use me for your ego-trips and ill-phrased political rants on Facebook again. They don't make sense. They've never made sense.

My attorney will be in contact.

Sincerely,
Your Samsung Galaxy S

* * *

PS- The government is eavesdropping on all of your phone conversations. Not that knowing will help you at this point.

DIAL-ME-AGAIN

Introducing Dial-Me-Again, the cell phone carrier for people who ask little of their life and less of their phone provider. Our service is like being marooned on an island and throwing a bottle with a message into the ocean and hoping the sharks don't send a note back to you that says, "You are so totally screwed."

What differentiates us from other carriers is our devotion to sketchy customer service, leaching off T-Mobile's network, consistently performing below the expectations you thought couldn't go any lower, and blah, blah, blah. You don't care. All you can hear is CHEAP, SAVE MONEY, NO MORE BIG COMPANIES, CANCÚN VACATION, BIG BOAT, RETIRE EARLY, CHA-CHING, CHA-CHING, CHA-CHING.

And that's why you'll come crawling to us. That's why you'll deal with our byzantine billing practices, scream at our two-person tech support team who learned English from a Toshiba DVD player manual, and spend more hours figuring out your voicemail than calling people. The altar of thrift is littered with the corpses of people just like you. It sounds dark now but by the end of your contract, you'll understand exactly what we mean.

Often you may wonder how to get reception on your bastardized device. It's simple. Go to the middle of Iowa, orientate yourself to the star Betelgeuse, gaze at your phone as if it decapitated your dog, mash the power button fifteen times in nine-second intervals, shove a pen into the charging port, and massage your phone's side in a counter-clockwise motion. Apologize for any wrongdoings you may have committed and promise to do better in the future. Compliment your phone in ways that are authentic and heartfelt.

After this, your phone may demand a six-hour update, or it may not—but it probably will. Unfortunately, this will destroy your hope and optimism when the update fails within minutes of completion and then ridicules you for even trying, like what Congress did to Obama.

After the update fails, your only option is to hold your phone over a glass of water and to shout profanity. Or you can drive to wherever the person you tried to call is and talk face-to-face. We like to think of reception issues as an invitation to a more personalized form of communication.

However, in an emergency—say you're trapped in a house with a serial killer or beating off bull sharks in the lower Zambezi or just *have* to have pizza—our phones are guaranteed to work. They are equipped with a "borrow someone else's phone" feature, which works with your nearest social contacts such as Mom, your son or daughter, a friend with an iPhone, the businessman who looks like Mr. Smith from the *Matrix*, the woman who failed to notice when "some perfume" became "enough perfume to fumigate a two-bedroom condo," and the guy who could probably find you some crack. Their phones almost always work, and you don't have to pay to use it. Sounds like a good situation to us.

Or choose to use your data and pop on the internet to send an email to 911. Something to the effect of: *Sharks developing increasingly complex tactics. Cannot bail water fast enough. They have already taken Jerry. Send help soon.* With our data limit, your emergency email should go through depending on multiple factors we won't go into here.

Of course, data goes fast, so fast you'll wonder if you had any to begin with. Should your data limit expire, we'll break into your house and plaster your car with bumper stickers advertising our phone service and then drain your account to an offshore bank where it will be used to buy lots and lots of big guns for bad people. Really bad people. It's all in the terms and conditions, which you threw away. HA HA HA. JUST TRY GETTING OUT OF OUR CONTRACT NOW.

At almost all times, you'll question why you won't pay money for an established phone service, but then—hand to God—your phone will work, and you'll have a pleasant conversation with your aunt, which almost never happens. It's those moments that our company stands for, those moments and skimming as much money as we can from this company before it careens downhill like a college freshman at a kegger.

For a limited time then, we ask you to start your slow descent into insanity. Choose Dial-Me-Again. Choose it now. Choose it before the logic center of your brain kicks in. Choose it forever.

HARRY POTTER AND THE OCCULT

After twenty years of research, scientists have concluded *Harry Potter* turns readers into worshipers of the occult, as can be noted by the inexplicable rise in the sacrifice of small helpless animals. Churches of the occult, previously found in basements and back alleys of Barnes And Noble bookstores, have been slowly infiltrating our institutions, resulting in legislation favoring Satan and malevolent mythical creatures.

One typical case is Little Timmy Shoemaker from Duluth, Minnesota. Within three months of reading *The Sorcerer's Stone*, Little Timmy had begun peddling possessed crucifixes to his classmates. During recess, he performed séances and preached the gospel of the chosen one to his classmates, soon causing "The Crayon Uprising." The rebellion was quelled but only after the use of tear gas and tranquilizer solution placed in the school's supply of milk.

No longer is *Harry Potter* solely for adolescents, however. The recent bipartisan passing of the American Witches And Wizards Act, which provides retirement and pension benefits for magicians nationwide, was traced to a Tuesday movie night in which several congressmen viewed *The Prisoner of Azkaban*. In a separate undercover investigation, several senators professed allegiance to Slytherin and were plotting the return of He-Who-Must-Not-Be-Named.

The recent publishing of *Satanism: The Bestest Religion Ever?* has been instrumental in the canonization of some of the more controversial elements of what has been deemed "Potterism." The components include the deification of J.K. Rowling, pilgrimage to Diagon Alley, daily prayers to Harry, Ron, and Hermione, and the complete destruction of the current world order.

The sudden surge in the purchase of fake wands, Death Eater insurance, and tall pointy hats is also traceable to a fascination with the occult. From its conception in 1997, the mega-store Spells-R-Us—not to be confused with Spells-R-Not-Us—has grown 67,000 percent, employing 20 percent of the US blue-collar workforce.

The most distinct area of growth is in the increase of computer hauntings. Demon possession in the pre-digital age resulted in individuals with their head rotated 180 degrees, crawling on the top of the ceiling, puking out copies of *The God Delusion*. But now any *Harry Potter* material on a computer may cause the device to dye its screen black, dabble in Ouija, and download vast quantities of emotionally-distraught punk rock.

These computers control the air defense of the eastern

seaboard, the voting records of every US citizen, Facebook, and much of England. In a recent development, the passwords to release the United States' nuclear weapons were changed to obscure characters in the Potter universe. Earth's fate now depends on whether the free world can remember the name of the guy who did that one thing, you know, with the spell.

It may be that you know someone who is a Potterist. Unfortunately, it's impossible to detect when a relatively benign Potterist has lost all psychiatric control and is plotting your murder. If you smell freshly baked cookies or detect a new brand of soap in the bathroom, it may already be too late. The best recourse is to counter their "book clubs" and costume parties with preemptory gunfire and ostracism.

One way to avoid accidental conversion is to reject *Harry Potter* books, movies, cultural references, magic, sticks that look like wands, griffins, centaurs, people who resemble Harry Potter, schools, and individuals with red hair. If you encounter Potterist material, immediately remove whatever part of your body has come in contact with the offending article.

If you have dabbled in Potterist literature yourself, please report to the nearest government office with a sign on your person that reads, "Please take away my dignity." You may be infected beyond all hope of recall. If you have developed a near irresistible attraction to Emma Watson or Daniel Radcliffe, you will be subject to a full body search and restricted to a straitjacket for the duration of your life.

Remember that all precautions and quarantine measures are for the safety of you and your loved ones. A free Potterist is a dangerous Potterist. A dangerous Potterist is a threat. Threats, especially those from fantastical novels, need to be dealt with.

THE FOOD STRUGGLE

A piece of broccoli is like a very small tree, which makes anyone eating it a giant. If you're ever feeling small, insubstantial, insignificant—and in terms of the universe, it's very hard not to feel that way—broccoli is your ticket out. Of course, trees taste terrible, unless you're a woodpecker... though woodpeckers don't *eat* wood, do they? Termites would probably be a better example, but termites are bugs and bugs are insignificant, unless you happen to be that exasperating ant in *A Bug's Life*. And that ant sucked.

Broccoli's sibling celery is like a small canoe—designed by an idiot. If you want to feel insignificant, celery would be the vegetable for you; it's the closest you can come to chewing mushy water with floss in it. No one should be surprised if celery was produced by a dentist in New Jersey, and his name was Dr. Worst Dentist Ever.

Rabbits don't actually like carrots; they like the color orange and the feeling of power. Rabbits also happen to be the cutest, hyperactive animal on the planet. They're like someone who could be nice to date until you discover the host of crippling insecurities just waiting for you to make a comment about their pants. Not that it's impossible to date someone like that, it's just harder when they bolt into the bushes when you move suddenly or throw a plate of rice at you because you mentioned neon leg warmers were *soooo* eighties.

French fries are the prostitutes of the potato world, and hash browns are the drug addicts—but it's hard not to fall into something destructive when you've been buried for three months and taste like a raw potato. Really, we should be surprised that yam turned out so well. Discrimination against the color orange isn't anything to scoff at.

The whole healthy world is upheld by the apple; they pay their taxes, get their bills in on time, go bowling every Friday night, and talk enthusiastically about the current weather. Not quite as exotic as a banana or zesty as an orange sure, but they get the job done. Tomatoes, on the other hand, are apples with a psychiatric disorder; ketchup is psychiatric tomato blood, and mustard... you don't want to know what mustard is. As far as pickles go, they're depressed cucumbers, and cucumbers are depressed zucchini. Zucchini's doing all right.

No one remembers to send okra a Christmas card, and they usually misspell "okra" anyways. Ocra? Akra? Okrah? Occasionally, someone visits her when they go south for spring break and feel obligated to drop by for an afternoon. The visit is… okay, nothing too catastrophic. She calls everyone Lenny for no explicable reason, has a creepy doll collection, and adopts homeless cats—or they're the neighbor's cats, and she stole them.

Green bean comes from a large family, none of whom like each other, even though they're all technically the same. Okay maybe not genetically but realistically—they're malnourished, hang around all day, and are unaccountably boring, like pretend-your-spoon-is-a-star-destroyer-shooting-down-rebel-scum-while-they-go-on-about-Gurdy's-hip-replacement boring.

Beans and peas are related and occasionally marry each other, which is why beans look a little like peas and also not like peas at all. Both beans and peas' genetics are all pretty much shot, and it's hard to understand who's related to whom when no one can put together a cohesive sentence. Their fiber, however, is off the charts.

Lime and lemon are sisters, though lime never quite left their parents' basement. Lemon, on the other hand, moved out and subsequently pissed off most everyone in her life. She's a bit of a sour character, though she's managed a living as a local barkeep and a garnish for fish and chips. Occasionally, she scores lime some gigs at bars. Neither has a boyfriend.

Orange and banana are friends, which is why they taste so good in smoothies. Banana is gay—and it's totally cool with all the other fruits—whereas kiwi is still figuring out who he is and what he feels. Is he really a large grape? Does he have some relation to orange? Why is carrot so attractive? *Sigh...* it's complicated, and it's going to take some time for kiwi to figure it out.

Pineapple is definitely not gay, not that he gets much action either way. It's hard to get past the fact that he could stab you with a bunch of spikes during a congenial bit of snuggling. But he lives in Hawaii and is pretty fine with where he is in life, so the whole situation's okay for him. Pineapple is also friends with orange and banana because, as mentioned before, the whole smoothie thing.

It doesn't take a genius to know that a corn cob is simply one kernel cloned eight hundred times. But it's all right because the original was a nice chap, and corn gets along with everyone. In fact, if it's possible to be too gregarious, corn would be pushing that line. You just can't be friends with Monsanto and expect to live a virtuous life. Monsanto is like the Corleone family of corn. *We gonna' make you an agricultural subsidy deal you can't refuse.*

Actually, if we could all imagine that our fruits and vegetables spoke with accents, we could go a long way to understanding the current nutrition situation, which is bad, very bad. Any casual eater should be on the watch. Never mind human relationships or your weight-loss goals, the relationships on your plate have never been so fractious and convoluted.

The amount of passive aggression in a normal serving of salad would be enough to kill a small squirrel. Merely mixing together cranberry sauce and mashed potatoes is a tacit approval of scorched-earth warfare. You could call the overall situation "The Food Struggle." It has persisted from generation to generation, through and with all the cultures of the world, and is coming soon to a plate near you.

AIRPORT SECURITY

Here are some important TSA tips for this upcoming holiday season—and hopefully, we won't have to use the electric fence this year.

At the very least, arrive at the airport fifteen to seventeen hours before your flight departs. Ideally, you will be at the airport soon after you have purchased your ticket and camp at the boarding gate for three months. This will give you enough time to sit, wait, and gaze at the vast, teeming masses of humanity in one of their most vulnerable states.

By the time you board, you will wonder what exactly you have in common with these creatures you once called "fellow citizens" and "friends," the same ones whom hunger and a two-hour plane flight has reduced to beings who would happily bargain your life for a peanut butter and jelly sandwich.

Should you have the unfortunate opportunity to be outside the United States for any period of time, having to deal with our friends in the Immigration Department will make sure you never leave again. The long lines of restless, testy citizens will confuse you, making you think that yes, this is the 1890s and no, immigration officer, I don't have cholera. I swear.

Under no circumstances should you attempt to smuggle in fruits, vegetables, or any animal byproducts, as the US customs form states, "Any fruit or vegetable not grown on American soil will single-handedly ensure the destruction of the US agricultural system." They are, of course, referencing the year 1901 when Hans Kindersproot decimated the tuber crop with several potatoes he brought on the eight-day sea voyage from Europe.

Once accepted into the best country in the world, you would think your troubles are over, but you would be wrong. Whatever shreds of your dignity the Immigration Department left whole, we—the all-powerful TSA—will deconstruct.

Going through security would seem to be a straightforward endeavor to protect our nation's security. But we like to spice things up on boring days like Christmas or Thanksgiving and understaff crucial security checkpoints, pushing you close to "setting off that goddamn bomb" yourself.

Thou shalt not have any water in a container, or the wrath of ye holy security team shall rain down upon thee. If we do our job well—and no guarantee on that—there will be no hydration on your flight, unless you manage to fill up a container by angling it into the miserable dribble of a drinking fountain, to which we respond, *Well played Mr. Kulashenko. We know an old commie trick when we see one. We'll be deporting you back to your socialist hellhole soon.*

Unfortunately, we usually see something suspicious in your backpack, a rounded object that might be a Frisbee but is more likely a complex thermonuclear detonation device. Oh, and we'll find that blunt pocket knife too. Sure, you could have left it there by accident, but with three screaming children and a leaking sippy cup, we bet your plans are to hijack that airplane on the way to Minneapolis.

The part we like best is where—after pawing through your personal items in blue safety gloves, as if you are a plague victim attempting to leave a quarantine area—we smash an object of our choice with a Patriot-Act-approved mallet. This procedure protects you from bad guys. No really.

We also have a new imaging technology that will scan your soul for any latent evil or ties to fascists/Al-Qaeda operatives/people who have complained about a parking violation. Please raise your hands in the air as if a police officer is frisking you and hope to God this equipment doesn't cause cancer. In fact, while you are in that position, say a few "Hail Marys" and think what it would like to be beaten and put on a cross.

What we really want is to say is that we persecuted a religious savior. It fits nicely between "protected American lives" and "got a little carried away with that beating stick" when we apply for a position at Guantanamo. But that's a couple years down the road. Right now, we just want to get through this holiday season without resorting to the cattle prod. So, try to remember these travel tips, and we'll try to remember your Miranda rights.

Appendix

KARATE KICK TUTORIAL

If someone attempts to take this book from you in a violent manner, this how to complete a karate kick. Make sure to ascertain whether or not this person is simply trying to borrow your book. If this is the case, reconsider kicking them—unless it's Justin. He never gives you anything back. It'll be the Crock-Pot incident all over again.

1. Think back to when you played soccer. If you didn't play soccer, think back to when you used to kick things. If you still kick things, you don't need this tutorial.

2. Go for the "shock and awe" technique. As any politician will tell you, this involves lots of blustering and occasionally bombing an innocent village. Yell, scream, threaten legal action. If you are loud enough, you will not have to proceed any further. If they do not back down, generally you will have to follow up what you've said and invade North Korea.

3. Aim for the head. If you are not that flexible, aim lower but not so low that it's embarrassing.

4. Let fly a foot of fury.

5. Rejoice.

FINDING THE MAN OR WOMAN OF YOUR DREAMS

Be yourself—but not the parts of you that suck.

Made in the USA
Monee, IL
24 September 2024